THE UNZIPPED GUIDES™
for everything you forgot to learn in school

Peterson's

Research Papers
UNZIPPED

Susan H. Stafford

PETERSON'S

A nelnet COMPANY

PETERSON'S

A **ⓝelnet** COMPANY

ISBN-13: 978-0-7689-2490-9
ISBN-10: 0-7689-2490-1

Printed in the United States of America

10 9 8 7 6 5 4 3 2 1   09 08 07

First Edition

MORE UNZIPPED GUIDES

Essays Unzipped
Newswriting Unzipped
Short Stories Unzipped
Speeches & Presentations Unzipped

CONTENTS

INTRODUCTION

THAT BLANK PIECE of paper is staring you in the face. It still hasn't filled up by itself. Inspiration hasn't struck yet. The clock is ticking. Your deadline is approaching. Getting a cup of coffee or a soda sounds like a good idea, but you've already used that excuse and a zillion others—watching *Star Trek* re-runs, washing your hair, downloading 4,000 new tunes to your iPod, and even doing chores—to put off the inevitable, the inescapable: writing your research paper.

You think you're doomed. You're going to get an "F," fail the entire course, flunk out of school, and ruin your future career as a video game designer, high-priced lobbyist, emergency room nurse, or investment banker. Your entire life is going down the tubes! You're coming unzipped before you've even started!

Don't hit the panic button. None of that's going to happen. Why? Because you're smart enough to read this book and find out how to ace your research papers. You'll learn an easy, step-by-step process from choosing a topic to writing the final paper that will help you zip through it. Let's get going.

CHAPTER 1

Unzipping the
Research Paper

LIKE PUBLIC SPEAKING, the words "research paper" can make your heart start to pound and knees knock together. Your mind suddenly goes blank. You're sure you'll never be able to write enough to fill even one page, much less ten or more.

Take a deep breath and relax. You do research every day when you surf the Internet looking for a good deal on video games or clothes. You almost write a paper in your head when you line up your reasons to persuade your folks to purchase that new 60-inch flat screen TV. Doing research and pulling a paper together takes time and some know-how, but once you understand the basics, you'll be able to impress your instructors—and maybe even yourself.

This chapter reveals:

- The Basics of the Research Paper

- Different Approaches to Research Papers

- Reasons to Write Your Own Work (Rather Than Borrow Others)

WHAT IT IS AND WHAT IT'S NOT

By now, you've had lots of assignments that require you to write some kind of paper for a class: a book report, an essay, a library report, or a term paper. These types of papers may require that you do some research, but they don't usually require the same depth, complexity, or creativity of a research paper. A true research paper "kicks it up a notch," as a famous chef would say.

For example, an **essay** is often a short composition that describes, analyzes, interprets, or argues an issue, often from the author's personal viewpoint or experience. It is called **expository writing** because its main purpose is to explain or interpret. The college admissions essay, for example, requires you to explain why you—out of all the other geniuses applying—should be allowed to grace the halls of this particular institution. An essay on the nature of patriotism might be based on your personal feelings about the subject. A five-paragraph essay is a typical classroom assignment, especially in English or literature class.

ZIP TIPS

Term Paper: The "term paper" is often used to refer to any type of writing assignment—an essay, report, or research paper—that's due at the end of the term or semester.

A typical **report** is the end-of-the-semester monster hiding in your mental closet that you try to avoid doing until the last possible minute. It's usually five to ten pages long and often focuses on a:

- Topic assigned by your instructor or drawn from the subject matter of the class

- Description of, or explanation about, the topic

- Summary of available materials or data on the topic

You're not required to do a lot of original thinking here—only to present information and show that you're able to pull together sources and thoughts in a logical, well-written manner. A typical report topic might be "The Causes of Global Warming" in which you describe and summarize existing theories about why the world seems to be heating up, with a concluding statement about the direction of future research.

A **research paper** ups the ante in terms of creativity and purpose. In a research paper, your instructor really wants to know your thoughts, see how far you can dig into primary and secondary sources, and be dazzled by how logically you can analyze or argue a topic. You've got a chance to combine creative thought with documentation to back up your point of view or analysis. A research paper can be five pages or up to several hundred pages, but your assignment will probably be one that requires between five and twenty-five pages.

A research paper focuses on:

- An original or assigned topic

- A main **thesis** or main point

- Your interpretation, evaluation, or argument

- The creative use of expert sources to persuade readers to support your analysis or argument

- Use and careful documentation of multiple sources

Long research papers that are written by candidates for an academic degree are often called **theses** (plural of thesis). Many high school or college honors programs require a senior or capstone thesis for graduation. Many graduate programs, especially master's degree programs, require a thesis. The "super-sized" graduate school research paper is the **dissertation**, the hallmark work for the Doctor of Philosophy degree or Ph.D.

REPORT, ANALYZE, OR ARGUE?

A research paper will usually require you to go beyond reporting, i.e., describing a situation or problem and summarizing it. You have to unzip your mind and be creative, and you have to develop your own point of view and support it with evidence. Research papers fall into two main types:

1. Analytical

2. Argumentative or persuasive

An **analytical research paper** requires that you pose a research question, critically examine and analyze a topic, and reach your own conclusion about the question you have posed. You're taking a close look at available sources, thinking creatively about what others have said, and coming up with your own special interpretation about, or perspective on, the materials.

An **argumentative** or **persuasive research paper** is the kind that is often required by instructors, especially in college. For this type of paper especially, you'll need to develop a thesis, or main point, and center your argument about it. Your research will focus on data, facts, statistics, opinions, and explanations that you will use to argue and support your point of view. Your goal in this type of paper is to persuade your readers to adopt the position you've taken.

In contrast to that report on the causes of global warming, a research paper will require you to zoom in on a specific aspect of global warming to be analyzed or argued.

ZIP TIPS

Good research papers address the questions: "How?" and "Why?" in addition to "Who?" "What?" "Where?" and "When?"

An analytical research paper, for example, can focus on the question of "The Role of Fossil Fuel in Global Warming," critically examine available research and arguments on the issue, and then present your perspective or conclusion about the contribution fossil fuel makes to heating up the environment.

An argumentative research paper on the topic of global warming can start with this main idea or thesis: *Global warming is a direct result of industrialized nations' assault on the environment with hydrocarbon fuels in the twentieth and twenty-first centuries* and build arguments to support that statement.

Think about it this way. If you only ask and answer the "Who?" "What?" "Where?" and "When?" questions, you're just reporting. If you add the "How?" and "Why?" questions, you've got the basic gist of the types of information and questions you'll need to construct a research paper with some punch to it.

TICK, TOCK: HOW MUCH TIME WILL THIS TAKE?

Of course, the answers to this question are: "That depends" and "Longer than you think."

If you've written on the topic before or happen to have some expert knowledge in your chosen subject, you're already ahead of the game. If you know zip, you'll need to plan some extra time to do preliminary research to get a grip on the topic and make sure your topic is not too big, not too small, but just right.

Make It Bite-Sized

One way to get a handle on time is to break the research paper down into bite-sized pieces and assign a timeframe to each piece. That way, the assignment doesn't look so overwhelming, and you can check off each step as you go. Expand and contract the following steps depending on how much time you have. Work backward from your due date, and be sure to build in one or two days for unexpected disasters.

Follow These Steps to Success

The 12 basic steps of researching and writing a research paper are:

1. Overcoming the shock once you hear about or remember the assignment. Try to limit your shock to 5–10 minutes rather than five to ten days.

ZIP TIPS

It's a given: No one ever has enough time to write a research paper, but planning ahead and leaving yourself extra time can take some stress out of the project.

2. Preliminary research to select a topic and begin a working **bibliography** (list of sources).

3. Zeroing in on a specific topic.

4. Writing a preliminary thesis statement.

5. Conducting your research and taking notes.

6. Making an outline for your first draft.

7. Writing a first draft.

8. Rooting out additional sources.

9. Completing your first draft with source materials cited.

10. Revising, editing, and proofreading.

11. Creating a final bibliography.

12. Pulling the final version together.

Remember to start early! Your instructor will not understand that you just had to enter and win that local foosball tournament or spend 10 hours a day glued to the tube watching reruns of *South Park* rather than tackling your paper and getting it done on time.

TO BUY OR NOT TO BUY? THAT IS THE QUESTION

You might have gotten your assignment at the beginning of the semester and thought you had a lot of time. Or, a short assignment might have popped up mid-semester. Either way, unless you've planned well, you're probably short on time.

With the clock ticking, you might be tempted to start searching for the easy way out: buying a paper online. Very tempting. You can indeed buy a paper that meets all the required specifications, has been written by really great writers who know their stuff (actually the stuff you should find out yourself), and will help you meet your deadline and your overwhelming desire to get an "A" without doing the work. What could be better?

What's better is for you to do your own work. Why not yield to temptation? Here are a few good reasons:

- *You're not learning anything if you let someone else do your work.* You've got a job—being a student and becoming educated. Doing your own assignments is one way of

ZIP TIPS

You'll spend about 60 percent of your time planning and researching a paper and 40 percent writing it. Set target dates for the completion of each step to keep yourself on course.

fulfilling your current job requirements. It's also good practice for the world beyond high school or college where you're expected to do your job if you want to get paid. Even if the course is snooze city, wake yourself up, find a topic that interests you, and write your own paper.

- *In the future, you'll need the skills that you'll learn writing a research paper.* No matter what your future job, you'll need excellent communication skills. Research papers teach you about writing, critical thinking, analysis, and integration of materials into a coherent document, as well as about ways to dig up the facts. Even a quick office memo needs to be persuasive.

- *Your instructors aren't stupid.* They've seen plenty of papers hot off the online manufacturing press. If they do know you personally, they'll know your style, tone, and capacity for writing and researching. Something that looks and sounds just too good to be you usually is identifiable as a "fake" to an instructor. Even if instructors don't know you, they're pretty savvy about the type of papers students in their classes can compose.

- *Plagiarism software exists, and it is designed to catch you.* The research paper Web site might claim that it does not recycle papers and everything's on the up and up, but why take that chance? With a few key strokes, your instructor might see that your "original" research paper has been used before or that substantial sections of your work have been swiped from a document on the Internet. End result: You've wasted your money and gotten yourself into a big mess!

HANDS OFF OTHERS' WORK!

Plagiarism sounds like a disease that you don't want to have . . . and it is. Plagiarism is basically cheating, and you don't want to be involved in it in any way, shape, or form. Plagiarism boils down to claiming someone else's work as your own and failing to give proper credit to the true source. Buying a paper, having someone else write a paper for you, borrowing a paper written by someone else, and copying a paper or article from a print or online source are all forms of plagiarism.

So, it might be tempting to pay a fee and download an "original" research paper from a Web site that sounds legitimate. It's still plagiarism, and it can get you kicked out of your class and kicked out of school.

UNZIPPING RIGHT ALONG

- Understand how your instructor uses the terms **essay, report, term paper,** and **research paper.**

- Understand what type of paper your instructor expects you to write. If it's not clear, ask!

- Put on your thinking cap and get ready to put your personal stamp on your research paper through a creative analysis, interpretation, evaluation, or argument of a topic.

- Plan out the steps you need to research and write your paper and leave enough time to accomplish each one. Keep yourself on track with due dates for completing each step.

HIDDEN SNAGS

- Deciding that you can slide by and turn in whatever type of paper you want, regardless of what your instructor requests.

- Skipping over important steps in thinking about, and writing, your paper. There's a logic to developing the research paper, and following those steps will make it easier to write one that merits an "A."

- Opting to buy a research paper online, borrow one, or have someone else write it for you. They're all dumb ideas and all are plagiarism.

HOOK ME UP TO MORE RESOURCES

There's more help out there. Many high schools and colleges have online writing institutes to take the mystery out of the research paper and help you succeed. In addition, your library or bookstore will have more in-depth, how-to books on this topic.

- Internet Public Library for Teens Teenspace: A+ Research & Writing, **www.ipl.org/div/teen/aplus,** has in-depth information on all facets of producing an excellent research paper.

- "Writing a Research Paper" at **http://owl.english.purdue. edu/workshops/hypertext/ResearchW/index.html** brings together the accumulated knowledge of Purdue University's Online Writing Center staff.

- *Online Research Guide* from Springfield Township High School's Virtual Library at **www.sdst.org/rguide** gives a great overview from the high school level.

MORE TO UNZIP

The point of the research paper is to teach you how to find relevant information, analyze it, think critically about how to build an analysis or support a position, and to write about what you've found out in a logical way, using correct English.

Believe it or not, these skills will help you in almost any future career. The ability to communicate clearly and effectively is a skill that employers value highly, especially as they find that very few employees can actually do it.

Planning ahead and doing your own work will give you a head start (and help avoid last-minute headaches or an overwhelming desire to buy or borrow a paper and potentially ruin your academic career) in the fine art of making a point persuasively.

- *Tackling the College Paper—Tips on Getting It Done and Getting the A.* Students Helping Students. Scott Grinsell and Nataly Kogan, eds. Natavi Guides. 2005. NY, NY: Penguin Group (USA) Inc. offers advice directly from students and professors.

CHAPTER 2

**Unzipping Your Mind:
Choosing a Topic**

ONE OF THE hardest parts of writing a research paper can be choosing a topic. Finding a topic requires thought and even a first round of research! If you're lucky, your instructor will offer you a range of possible topics to get started. If not, you're on your own. You'll need to unzip your mind and start those ideas flowing.

The chapter reveals how to:

- Select a Topic

- Get a Focus: The Main Point (Thesis)

- Do Preliminary Research

LISTEN UP: WHAT'S THE ASSIGNMENT?

Your first step—understanding the assignment—is a critical one for success. If you blow it, you'll waste a lot of time in cyberspace and elsewhere aiming at the wrong target. Some foolproof methods of getting a grip on the assignment are:

- *Read the course outline and assignments.* Your instructor will indicate here how many papers are due and when. There may even be a list of suggested topics that relate directly to the course, plus instructions and details about format, required style for the bibliography, citations, etc., and the paper's required length.

- *Be there!* Chances are your instructor will discuss his or her expectations about the research paper, answer questions, and give other important details in class. If you're not there, you won't have the information firsthand. Depending on classmates is okay, but who's to say they got it right. It's better for you to hear the instructions yourself.

- *Take notes.* If you sit in class daydreaming, you're going to miss a lot, including material covered in class, possible research topics related to that material, and what your instructor finds important. Taking notes not only gives you something to do, it also gives you a permanent record and may give you a head start on your paper.

- *Get into your instructor's head.* Some instructors are more flexible than others about assignments and what they expect. If you've taken several courses with one specific instructor, you'll have a good idea of his or her likes and dislikes. If not, talking to your instructor about possible topics and the assignment can help you understand what is required. Instructors like to be consulted, so don't hesitate to make an office appointment!

UNZIP YOUR MIND: GET A TOPIC

What should you write about? If your instructor has chosen the topic for you or has given you several choices, that makes your life easier. If not, the field is wide open and you're in control. If the topic has to be closely related to the subject of the course, keep that in mind as you pick your brain and other sources.

To start, brainstorm a bit about general subject areas that interest you. Are you an athlete who knows all the stats about every player on your favorite team? Are you a couch potato who's into television? Do you crave to know about the latest fashion trends? If so, you've just identified a **subject,** a general field of knowledge that interests you: sports, television, or the fashion industry.

Unless you never want to finish your research paper, you'll have to narrow that subject down into a **topic,** a more specific aspect of the general subject in question. For example, a particular topic in television might be the industry's rating system, parental use of the V-chip, or the impact of cable television on the industry. If you're interested in sports, a topic could be the role and impact of professional athletes on the Olympic Games or the controversy over performance-enhancing drugs.

One way to start scoping out topics from a general subject is to list the subject, ask yourself what interests you about that subject area, and then start listing potential topics related to that subject area. Most likely, the first round will be rather broad, but you're eventually going to narrow the topic down more as you do your preliminary research.

More Examples of Possible Subjects and Topics	
Subject	**Topics**
Economy	Consumerism
	National Debt
	Impact of the Internet
Education	Community College
	Distance Education
	Admissions Policies
Environment	Global Warming
	Conservation Movements
	Tsunamis
Health	Eating Disorders
	Sports Medicine
	HIV/AIDS
Politics	The 2004 Election
	The British Parliamentary System
	Women World Leaders
Sports	Super Bowl
	The Olympics
	Professional Golf

You get the drift, but if you're still having trouble, here are some other steps you can take to start the ideas flowing.

Got Zip?

If you come up with zip by looking at your personal interests, stimulate your brain by thumbing through newspapers or magazines, watching the news, listening to the radio, reviewing the course material and texts, or going to the library and letting your fingers do the walking through the print or online catalog, databases, and reference books. Take a look at an online encyclopedia, such as *Wikipedia*, *Encyclopedia Britannica*, or *Encarta*, for inspiration. Sooner or later, you'll find something that sparks your interest.

Still Got Zip?

If you're really panicked, bat around a few ideas with your classmates, your instructor, or the teaching assistant. Ask your mom, dad, even your bothersome brother, sister, or roommate to brainstorm with you.

ZIP TIPS

Search for a general subject area *and* a suitable topic within that subject area at the same time.

Zip 'Em Up!

As ideas start popping out of your head, be sure they don't get away. Get a small notebook to carry with you and keep a list (that way all your ideas are in one place), draw cartoon balloons and fill in each balloon with an idea, keep a running log on your computer or PDA, stick a list on your refrigerator or bathroom mirror—anything to be sure those ideas don't escape.

NARROW YOUR FOCUS

Okay, you've zoomed in on a subject and a more specific topic that interests you; you'll still need to develop a more specific focus. This requires some thinking to further unzip the topic. Reference books, especially encyclopedias, give you a quick overview of a general subject or a topic and help you understand specialized vocabulary and key concepts. They are a good starting point for narrowing your search, especially if you don't know much about the topic.

Let's look at some of our topics again. You already know that you're not going to write a paper about sports because the subject matter is too broad. But each of the topics—the Super Bowl, the Olympics, professional golf—also has too much information zipped up in each category for your purposes. But, you are getting closer.

By identifying questions that interest you about a topic, you can identify some **subtopics** and start the creative juices flowing about your research question or thesis statement.

1. Why and how has the Super Bowl assumed such importance in the national psyche?

2. Does the city where the Super Bowl is played really benefit economically?

3. How has the media shaped the national obsession with the Super Bowl?

Subject	Topic	Subtopic
Sports	Super Bowl	Marketing the Super Bowl
		Impact on Local Economy
		History of the Super Bowl
		The Media and the Super Bowl

ZIP TIPS

Find some key words in reference books that relate to your topic. They will help you zero in on the topic both now and later with your future research.

Within the health subject area and topic of eating disorders, you can pose the following more specific questions to zero in on a more specific topic:

1. What are the most common eating disorders?

2. Are gender and age related to eating disorders?

3. What is the media's role in promoting or deterring eating disorders?

4. Is anorexia a physical or psychological problem or both?

5. Is obesity an addiction?

Subject	Topic	Subtopic
Health	Eating Disorders	Anorexia
		Bulimia
		Obesity
		Food and Addiction
		Adolescents and Eating Disorders
		The Media's Role in the Cult of Thinness

MAKE SURE YOUR TOPIC MAKES SENSE

Some questions to ask yourself about your potential topic:

- *Do I like the topic?* If your topic puts you to sleep, chances are it will also be snooze city for others. Why?

Because you'll find doing the research is a drag, and you won't be able to write about it with any enthusiasm. If, after doing some preliminary research, you don't like the initial topic you selected, choose a new one.

- *Is this worth writing about?* A topic like "Boozin' and Snoozin': Life in a Fraternity House" might be really amusing to you and your friends, but can you really turn it into a serious research paper? Ask: "Why does this matter?"and "Who cares?"

- *Is my topic too broad or too narrow?* You'll need to expand or contract your topic according to the requirements of your assignment. If you choose something too narrow, such as "The Merits of the Night Crawlers as Bait" and you need a twenty-page paper, you'll be scrambling to fill up the pages. Or, vice versa. It's unlikely that "The Fall of the Roman Empire" will fit in a five-pager. You may have to either expand or narrow your topic.

- *Do I have enough time to write a paper on this topic?* If you've only got two weeks, you need to be sure that your topic isn't so broad that you'll run out of time. Remember research and writing will both take more time than you think.

- *What information sources are available to me?* If you have access to a good library, take a quick look through its catalog and online databases to see what's already been written. You'll get a good idea of whether or not you'll be able to find enough information about your topic and if a diversity of sources is available.

- *Can I present a controversial subject sensitively?* Some hot topics, such as child pornography or alleged war crimes, need to be handled carefully. Be sure you can examine and argue a subject appropriately.

GET A POINT OF VIEW: START TO DEVELOP YOUR THESIS

Most research papers require that you either analyze or argue a point of view. This is where the concept of the thesis comes in. The thesis is the main idea or point of your paper. It is a clear assertion about something, states your position, is narrow enough to be supported by evidence, and usually only has one main point. You want your thesis to engage your audience and provoke thought or discussion. A thesis can argue, analyze, explain, or suggest a solution to a problem. It's important because your supporting ideas and evidence from your research will all relate to this main idea.

Let's say you decide to write about obesity in the United States.

No Thesis Here!

- *Americans are overweight.*

This is a fact or observation.

- *This paper is about obesity in the United States.*

This is the topic of your paper, but it is not the main point to be analyzed or argued.

- *Americans are overweight for many reasons.*

This statement does not give the reader an idea about what your position is and is too broad, especially if you are writing a short paper.

Here's a Thesis!

- *The epidemic of obesity in American society is a direct result of the government's failure to regulate the fast food industry and educate the public about the dangers of being overweight.*

ZIP TIPS

A good thesis is a one-sentence summary of your entire paper. It makes its purpose clear and gives your reader an understanding about its main ideas and the direction you're taking.

This statement is clear, states the purpose of the paper and what's to follow, can provoke differences of opinion about the cause of obesity (poverty, lack of education about nutrition, failure to exercise, etc.), and takes a stand by pointing the finger at the government.

No Thesis Here!

- *The Super Bowl generates income for the city where it is played.*

This is a fact or observation.

- *This paper will discuss the impact of the Super Bowl on the local economy of the city where it is played.*

You're close, but not a winner. This sentence simply states the paper's topic.

- *The Super Bowl affects the local economy of the city where it is played in many ways.*

Hmmm, still no idea of what the main point of your argument or analysis will be.

Now You've Got a Thesis!

- *The Super Bowl has a limited positive economic impact on the city where it is played, because much of the revenue generated is not reinvested in the local economy but is dispersed nationally.*

You've narrowed down your topic, taken a debatable position, and focused on one major point for your paper.

Your thesis statement will probably not spring completely formed from your head. You'll start with a working thesis and, as you do your initial research, you may expand or narrow it, depending on what materials you find. Don't think of it as something set in stone. You'll refine it over time.

UNZIPPING RIGHT ALONG

- Pay attention in class. If your instructor assigns a topic and gives specific instructions about how to write that paper, stick to it.

ZIP TIPS

If you can't state your thesis clearly in one sentence, you probably don't have one.

Research Papers **UNZIPPED**

- Let your mind wander, but not too much. Settle on a subject area and topic that interest you and have potential interest for your audience. Dazzle yourself and your instructor with your creativity.

- Be able to present your thesis in one clearly stated sentence that reveals your purpose—one main point to be examined or argued.

HIDDEN SNAGS

- Not asking your instructor to clarify an assignment if you don't understand it.

- Choosing a topic that's too broad—or too narrow. You'll either have to write an encyclopedia or you won't have enough to say.

- Failing to ask your instructor if you can expand the list of topics assigned in class if you have a different idea.

HOOK ME UP TO MORE RESOURCES

- **http://www.libraryspot.com/features/paperfeature.htm** has tips on how to identify a topic.

- **http://infodome.sdsu.edu/research/guides/hot/supersites. shtml** hooks you into major sites for potential topics with some zip at San Diego State University's "Subject Guide for Hot Topics Supersites."

- **http://www.lib.odu.edu/libassist/idea/index.php** (Old Dominion University Libraries Idea Generator) shows how a university online library can help you brainstorm.

- **http://www.indiana.edu/~wts/pamphlets.shtml,** from Indiana University, Bloomington, has an excellent

MORE TO UNZIP

In this chapter, you've learned how to get a grip on some of the toughest parts of the research paper: your topic and thesis. Unless your instructor has suggested some specific topics, they won't fall out of the sky. You'll need to unzip your brain and start letting ideas flow. Sources of inspiration include your own interests, brainstorming with others, talking with your instructor, preliminary research online or in the library, and other external sources of stimulation such as magazines or the news. Once you've chosen a general subject area, you'll narrow it down to a topic that interests you and develop a thesis or main point that will form the core of your research paper.

pamphlet on "How to Write a Thesis Statement," along with other pamphlets about writing.

- **http://www.esc. edu/esconline/across_esc/writerscomplex. nsf/home** (SUNY Empire State College's Writer's Complex) has exercises designed to help you improve your ability to select a good research question or thesis and to test whether or not a topic can be researched.

CHAPTER 3

**Unzipping Your Resources:
Doing the Research**

YES, A RESEARCH paper requires time and effort. By now, you know it's going to take more than a quick look through an encyclopedia or a reference book and some thinking to get this baby going. You'll need to do some digging to find your topic, narrow your focus, get a main point, and then support that point with facts and figures from a variety of sources.

There's so much information out there that you need to be smart about conducting your research, or you'll be so lost in an avalanche of facts, figures, and opinions that you won't be able to dig yourself out. You also want to be sure that the information you're collecting for use your paper is credible, so you'll need to know how to evaluate your sources.

This chapter reveals:

- Differences among Source Materials

- Available Sources of Information

- Effective Ways to Conduct Research and Evaluate Materials

PRIMARY AND SECONDARY SOURCES

A **primary source** is just what it sounds like: direct or firsthand information, straight from the source, at the time an event occurred. Interviews, original manuscripts, diaries or personal journals, autobiographies, surveys, historical documents or records, plays, poems, novels, newspaper articles written when an event occurs, films, and a radio or television broadcast are all examples of primary sources of information.

You can also create your own primary sources. For example, if you are doing a research paper on video games and you interview the founder of a video game company or someone who tests video games, those interviews are great primary sources of material that will add zip to your paper.

A **secondary source** is one step removed from a primary source. These sources are documents such as encyclopedias, biographies, textbooks, or newspaper or journal articles that are based on indirect knowledge or information. A biography of the video game company founder would be an example of a secondary source. An autobiography by the founder is a primary source.

HIT THE STACKS: THE LIBRARY

Libraries aren't what they used to be: stacks of dusty old books and periodicals (magazines, journals, and newspapers) with rabbit-eared library cards stuffed into catalog drawers. Most libraries and librarians are on the high-tech bandwagon with online catalogs of their holdings, so it's easier to locate materials for your paper.

Online Info

Take the Web site of the New York Public Library (NYPL) for example. On the opening page, www.nypl.org, there's access to a treasure trove of information:

- The LEO catalog of books and materials that can be checked out

- The CATNYP catalog for research books and materials

- An online database of magazines, journals, and encyclopedias that allows you to find articles

- A catalog of archives and manuscripts

- eNYPL, with downloadable books, music, and video for PCs, laptops, or portable devices

If the subject of comic books appeals to you as a cool topic for a research paper on graphic forms of literature, the NYPL online

ZIP TIPS

Both primary and secondary sources are valuable in your research and may be required by your instructor for your research paper. Instructors evaluate your sources, as well as your paper. Be sure to check if there is any limitation on the use of or number of sources from the Internet.

research catalog for the Humanities and Social Sciences Library can give you a great overview of materials held and additional sources:

- Selected Internet sites such as Classic Comic Books, Comics Research Bibliography, Michigan State Universities Libraries: Comic Art Collection

- Comic books in Microformats held by the library in the General Research Division; available print versions

- Books on artists, authors, and creators of comic books

- Works on the history and criticism of comic books and abstracts telling you about the books' contents

- Bibliographies and guides to comic books

- Encyclopedias

- Alternative search terms for comic books such as graphic novels, caricature and cartoons, and cartoonists

This research catalog also tells you what the library doesn't have: many original comics before 1960 and periodicals about comic books.

Printed Info

You can search a library's online or card catalog by title, author, word, or subject matter. All books in libraries have been sorted into fiction and nonfiction. Fiction books usually are arranged by author, whereas nonfiction books are classified by the Dewey Decimal system, Library of Congress system, or some other classification system that is based on subject matter. Books are given a call number, which identifies a specific book and allows you or the librarian to find it easily on the shelves. Books on similar subjects are grouped together.

In addition to their regular book collection, libraries are also a treasure trove of government documents; reference books such as encyclopedias, indexes, almanacs, and abstracts; atlases; pamphlets; and periodicals, such as academic journals, magazines, and newspapers.

Special Services

Libraries also offer many special services, such as interlibrary loan and free access to some databases, as well as special materials

ZIP TIPS

Think outside the tried-and-true resource box! Local historical societies, museums, professional associations, and similar organizations can all be great sources of materials for your research paper.

including audiovisuals, such as slides, records, cassettes, CDs, or photographs; and specialized collections, such as maps, local historical documents, or rare manuscripts.

One of the best parts about libraries is that there's a real live person there to help you. Librarians, especially reference librarians, are also experts in research and often in a content area, such as history. Consult them! They can help you get started or unstuck if you hit a snag in your research.

DIG INTO DATABASES

The good news is there are many excellent online databases, such as LexisNexis, a rich source of news and legal and financial information, and OCLC FirstSearch, which offers access to many

ZIP TIPS

Academic journals are great sources of information. Online or CD-ROM indexes, such as the *Reader's Guide to Periodical Literature*, the *Social Science Citation Index*, and *Arts and Humanities Citation Index*, contain information on articles published in these journals.

databases, scholarly articles, and library holdings. The bad news is that many of them charge a hefty annual fee or a fee per article. Others offer some information for free but add a charge or require a subscription for more detailed information. For example, www.hoovers.com, a rich source of information on corporations, will allow you to access a general profile of a business but will only allow subscribers to access detailed information about corporate officers.

If you don't have deep pockets, don't despair. Libraries often subscribe to special online databases, covering such topics as literature, the arts, social science, and so on, that you can access for free—they've already paid the fee! The New York Public Library, for example, offers users access to over 300 databases. Your local library might not offer that many, but chances are it will subscribe to at least some well-known databases.

What a deal! Within these subscription databases, you'll also have access to periodicals, reference books, and other special materials known to be published by reputable sources (they have already been examined for content and reliability by the database creators). The librarians have also reviewed and evaluated the databases for content, ease of use, relevance to library users, and so on.

SURF THE NET AND THE WEB

People frequently use the words "Internet" and "Web" interchangeably, but they refer to two distinct aspects of electronic information. The Internet is really a huge network of networks all linked together to give you access to information from around the world. The

World Wide Web refers to the roadways or pathways through the Internet. It's like a series of electronic pages in the huge electronic book called the Internet.

The Internet and the Web can be your friends and enemies at the same time. Friends because they help you access information instantly to get an overview of what's out there. Enemies because there's so much information out there that you can easily become overwhelmed instead of finding the specific research relevant to building your case. Their content also changes daily, so what's here today can be gone tomorrow! There's no big Librarian in the Sky cataloging all the material on the Web or a Super Editor enforcing standards for quality. What you find is what you get.

ZIP TIPS

You'll obviously need a library card to take out books, but you may also need one to access the library's online catalog offsite, subscription-only databases, or special research collections.

To do your research, you'll be searching for and retrieving World Wide Web pages on the Internet using a:

- *Metasearch engine*, such as www.webcrawler.com or www.dogpile.com (yes, that's correct), that allows you to retrieve results from multiple search engines simultaneously. Metasearch engines save you some time going from search engine to search engine by compiling results in one place.

- *Web directory,* such as Yahoo!, which classifies information by subject matter similar to a library (many directories also have search engines). A Web directory is especially helpful in getting an overview of, or general information about, a topic.

ZIP TIPS

Databases available through the library can save you time by taking you directly to credible sources instead of just "googling" a topic on the Web, a process that might net you more useless, rather than useful, sources.

- *Search engine*, such as Google, MSN Search, or Ask.com, which allows you to search by punching in a key word or phrase and then sends out inquiries to the Web. Search engines are particularly helpful if you already have a well-defined topic in mind because they allow you to zero in on it.

ADD SOME ZIP TO YOUR RESEARCH METHODS

Conducting research on the Web takes practice. If you're doing a paper on the influence of The Bill and Melinda Gates Foundation on HIV/AIDS in Africa and you type "Bill Gates" into a Web directory, you'll have instant access to a gazillion associated Web pages with information about Bill Gates—one search brought up 1,880,000 entries or **hits!** Narrow your search to "The Bill and Melinda Gates Foundation," and you'll have more targeted information about the foundation (30,100 hits). If you type in "The Bill and Melinda Gates Foundation AND HIV/AIDS," you'll focus in on the foundation's specific work on this issue and external documents related to it, such as newspaper articles or commentary about the foundation's work (25 hits).

To help you filter information, most search engines allow you to conduct what is called a **Boolean search** using the terms "AND" (includes both terms) or "OR" (searches for one or the other) or "NOT" (excludes a term). Web sites will usually have their own instructions for conducting an advanced search (based on the Boolean search). Follow those instructions to make your search easier and more rewarding.

Don't get discouraged if you don't hit paydirt with your first search terms. Try some synonyms or different combinations of words to change what comes up. For example, for your comic book search, try "comics," "comic books," "graphic novels," "cartoons," and "caricatures." Try a phrase such as "comics in the 1950s" or "comics as literature" to expand your search.

SEZ WHO? EVALUATE YOUR SOURCES

There's tons of information available in print and on Web sites, but how do you know it's accurate, reliable, or credible? On the Internet especially, anyone can post data or materials and make claims of expertise or authenticity. For print materials, you also need to ask yourself similar questions about the source and information presented. It's your job to sort it all out.

ZIP TIPS

Bookmark sites or add to your favorites' list those Web sites that look promising for more detailed investigation. That way, you'll be able to find them later.

The last thing you want to do in your research paper is to try to support your position with incorrect information or with a source that will make your instructor howl with laughter. An article about the feeding habits of sharks by famed oceanographer Jacques Cousteau has credibility. An online blog from a guy whose only experience is a near-miss as lunchmeat for a shark isn't going to cut it.

Test out the material with some of these questions:

- Where and how did you come to this information on the Web or in print? Did you start off with a known or reliable source?

- Who is the author? Are his or her credentials listed and what are they? Is this person cited by other sources or scholars known to be experts in the field?

- How recent is the information? Does the timeframe of the information suit your research purposes? Is the Web site where you found the information updated often? Is the information copyrighted?

- Does the author cite sources in his or her work to back up factual materials, claims, or opinions?

- If the author represents an organization, is there information about the organization and its mission, history, and board of directors available?

- Can you find out anything else about the author or organization, such as other publications, affiliations or, articles through other Web sites or in print?

UP CLOSE AND PERSONAL: DOING YOUR OWN RESEARCH

If you're a bit adventurous (or your instructor requires it) and you have time, doing you own firsthand research can be fun. You can unzip your lips and opt to conduct interviews or do a survey. For a sociology or anthropology paper on the impact of immigration on the family, for example, you might dig into your own family history, interview your own family members, and include their quotations and observations in your paper.

Another type of research common in social science courses is the survey where you design a series of questions about a topic and

ZIP TIPS

Just because it's on the Web doesn't mean it's true! Evaluate your online sources just like you'd evaluate those in print.

pose those questions to a designated group of individuals. Or, you may be asked to incorporate firsthand observations about people's behavior in your paper.

Of course, if you're in a science or psychology course, you may be required to design a research experiment and report your results. This type of research often follows a strict protocol and has its own format, so check on those details with your instructor.

These types of in-person research require some additional time—questionnaires or plans of action need to be developed, careful records need to be kept of conversations or observations, and time needs to be devoted to reviewing your notes. You'll definitely need to allow yourself sufficient time to do this "upfront" work for firsthand research.

ZIP TIPS

Colleges and universities often have institutional rules about conducting research with human, as well as animal, subjects. Make sure you know and follow those rules.

UNZIPPING RIGHT ALONG

- Know and follow your instructors' requirements for the inclusion of primary and secondary sources in your research paper.

- Get help with your research from your local librarian. Even if you think you're a whiz at research, you can learn some tips from the pros.

- Use relevant research from multiple sources, including the library. The Web has a lot of information, but not everything is available online.

HIDDEN SNAGS

- Relying on just one or two sources of information for your paper. You won't show your instructor that you know how to conduct research. You'll only prove you're incredibly lazy.

- Not taking a minute to read "Helpful Search Tips" in a Web directory or on a search engine site. You can search more efficiently and quickly if you know the rules.

- Spending way too much time searching the Web without yielding specific information needed for your paper. Give yourself a deadline for your search on a topic. If nothing— or too much—comes up and you can't narrow it down, it might be time to look for another topic.

HOOK ME UP TO MORE RESOURCES

- Sometimes, it's hard to distinguish between primary and secondary sources. Practice unzipping the two source types by taking a quiz from the SUNY Empire State College Writer's Complex at **www.esc.edu/htmlpages/ writerold/exer6.htm.**

MORE TO UNZIP

There's a lot of knowledge out there, so you have to be smart about how you use your time finding the information that you need. Although we like to think that everything has been computerized, digitized, or somehow made available via the Internet and on the Web, there's still a lot that's not, especially historic documents, recent books, and so on. It would be a shame to miss an important source because you didn't want to take a trip to the library.

Starting at your local library can be a big help, especially in getting a general overview of what types of documentation are available. You can search many library catalogs online, but seeing a reference librarian who is already a crackerjack researcher can really point you in the right direction.

Understand and use primary (firsthand) resources and secondary resources (those that are once removed from the original source) to give your paper flair. Make sure you give some thought to the credibility and validity of your printed and electronic resources.

- The Internet Public Library **(www.ipl.org)** and the Virtual Public Library **(http://virtualpubliclibrary.com)** allow you to explore different subject categories.

- The Library of Congress **(www.lcweb.loc.gov),** the National Archives **(www.archives.gov),** and the United States Department of Commerce **(www.fedworld.gov)** offer access to one of the world's great libraries and archives and will get you started if you need help accessing government information and documents.

- NoodleQuest **(http://www.noodletools.com/noodlequest/)** can help you identify search engines appropriate to your research goals. A small fee is required, but if you write a lot of research papers, it could be worth it.

- Evaluating sources, especially those from cyberspace, can be equally challenging. For more helpful tips, check out the University of Michigan's site: **http://www.lib. umich.edu/ugl/guides/evaluation.**

CHAPTER 4

**Unzipping Your Info:
Getting Organized**

AS YOU GO through the research process, you'll be collecting lots of information that you'll want to have handy. And putting it all on sticky notes that will only attach themselves to your elbow or disappear out the door stuck to your dog's rear end is not an option!

Unless you have a photographic memory, you'll need a system for easily organizing and accessing your data. Otherwise, your research will be as messy as your bedroom. You'll also waste hours hunting down that one critical missing piece of information or having a panic attack because you can't find the right source citation 3 minutes before your masterpiece is due.

This chapter reveals:

- Simple Ways to Document Your Research

- Essentials of Organizing Your Info

- Methods for Dealing with Too Much or Too Little Info

KEEP TRACK OF YOUR SOURCES

During your preliminary research, you don't need to take scads of notes, but you do need to make complete notations about books, periodicals, audiovisual materials, CDs, DVDs—whatever documents you think will be useful in writing your paper. If you don't write down the source somewhere now, you won't be able to find it later.

To start a preliminary list of sources or a **working bibliography,** you'll need some regular index cards. If you don't want to handwrite bibliography cards, type the information for each source on the computer. You can keep a separate page for each source under a folder entitled "Bibliography" and then print them out and rearrange them when you need them. Or, print out the info and then paste it on a regular index card. Use whatever method works best for you.

The basic bibliographic information you'll need to record for a book is:

- Title of the book

- Author's or editor's full name

ZIP TIPS

Use one paper or electronic card *per source* so you can reshuffle them later when you want to put your sources in alphabetical order.

- Date and place of publication

- Edition of the book

- Publisher

- The book's library call number (and name of library where you found it if you go to more than one)

- Web site URL if you've accessed an electronic book online

- Date you accessed the electronic book online

For an article from a periodical, such as a magazine, journal, or newspaper, you'll need:

- Author

- Title of the article

- Name of the periodical

- Date the article was published

- Volume number

- Page numbers (as available)

- URL for an online journal or periodical, name of the site, date you accessed the site

A good rule of thumb for Internet/Web sources is to have the following information:

- Name of the author or organization

- Date of the electronic publication or latest update

- Full title

- Description of the type of document, such as listserv or newspaper

- URL

- Date you accessed the material

Other Formats

Audiovisual material, CDs, DVDs, and so on will need much the same information as printed material, plus the dates and times that the materials were produced.

Interviews

For any interviews you conduct, be sure to make a similar card with all the relevant contact information: name, address, telephone number, e-mail address, plus the date, time, and subject of the interview.

E-mail

Document all information received by e-mail with name, date, time, and subject matter so that you know who said what and when. Better yet, copy the e-mail on your computer or file it in an e-mail folder online.

CITE IT RIGHT!

As already noted, there are many different ways to document your sources. You could create your own system, but if you follow an established method, you'll have a much easier time creating your bibliography, endnotes, and footnotes.

Become familiar with one or more of the style manuals, as they are called, as you build a bibliography and take notes. You'll be less likely to run screaming from your room in frustration or to dive into a quart of chocolate ice cream to console yourself when you can't find the precise reference later in the writing process.

Each style manual requires basically similar information for your sources but differs in the presentation format. Some of the most

ZIP TIPS

Assign a number to each of your sources or create a way to code your sources by type, such as B1, B2 for books or A1, A2 for articles. When you make your note cards, put the source code or number on the note card rather than rewriting the entire bibliographic information.

commonly used style manuals for formatting your paper and documenting and citing sources are:

- *MLA* (Modern Language Association) *Style Manual and Guide to Scholarly Publishing* (for the humanities and liberal arts)

- *The Chicago Manual of Style* (for history and other disciplines)

- *The Publication Manual of the American Psychological Association* (for psychology and other social sciences)

Remember there are specific formats for each type of printed or electronic documents: books, encyclopedias, indexes, periodicals, pamphlets, government documents, CD-ROMS, audiovisual materials, and so on. Be sure to consult a reference book to get each format right!

Also remember that these well-known style manuals don't have a hammerlock on how to cite and document your sources. Some disciplines, such as sociology or engineering, also have style manuals that your instructor may prefer to follow.

WRITE IT DOWN

After you've done some preliminary reading, gotten a focus for your paper, and have a working bibliography together, you'll want to dig deeper into your sources. This is the time to start taking

Presentation Format Examples

	Print Book (One Author)	Print Article	Online Document
Modern Language Association	Author's last name, first name. *Book title*. Place of publication: Publisher, Year of publication. Kent, Clark. *How I Learned to Fly*. New York: OutofSight Books, 2007.	Author's last name, first name. "Title of article." *Publication* Date: page numbers. Kent, Clark. "It's a Bird. It's a Plane. It's Just Me!" *OutofSight Magazine* 3 Jan. 2000: 31–35.	Author's last name, first name (if available). *"Title."* Publication date. Date of access, <Web address> Kent, Clark. *"My Autobiography."* 25 January 2007. 2 February 2007. <http: //www.clark.net>
Chicago Manual of Style	Author's last name, first name. *Book title*. Place of publication: Publisher, Year of publication. Kent, Clark. *How I Learned to Fly*. New York: OutofSight Books, 2007.	Author's last name, first name. Article name in quotations marks. Source in italics, volume (date): page numbers. Kent, Clark. "It's a Bird. It's a Plane. It's Just Me!" *OutofSight Magazine* 12 (January 3, 2000): 31–35.	Author's last name, first name. Name of document in quotation marks. Available from: http://xxx, accessed day/month/year. Kent, Clark. "My Autobiography." Available from http://www.clark.net; accessed 2 February 2007.
American Psychological Association	Author's last name, first initial. (Year of publication). *Book Title*. Place of publication: Publisher. Kent, C. (2007). *How I Learned to Fly*. New York: OutofSight Books.	Author's last name and initials. (Year of publication). Title of article. *Periodical name, volume*, page numbers. Kent, C. (2000). It's a Bird. It's a Plane. It's Just Me!. *OutofSight Magazine, 12*, 31–35.	Author's last name, initials. (Date of work). *Title of work*. Retrieved month day, year, from source. Kent, C. 2007, January 25 *My Autobiography*. Retrieved February 2, 2007, from www.clark.net.

notes. Whether they're neatly handwritten or typed, your well-documented notes will be your best friends while pulling your paper together.

Do It by Hand

The good old 3 × 5 (or slightly larger 4 × 6) index card is a tried-and-true method for taking notes. Rather than writing everything in a spiral notebook in a steady stream, note cards allow you to put a discrete quotation or piece of information on a single card with a topic or subtopic heading. You'll easily be able to organize and sort your cards by topic or subtopic when you start your paper, lay out the analysis or argument, and look for supporting information.

The card method also saves you from rifling through sheets and sheets of paper and re-reading every single note as you try to find

ZIP TIPS

Your instructor may have a preferred method of documenting and citing sources and may give you a style sheet. Use the one your instructor assigns or prefers to make up your bibliography cards and notes.

that one important fact: Was it 3,000 or 300,000 species that have become extinct in the life span of humankind?

Here's what a well-written note card looks like:

Call No: XXX Child Labor—Demographics (Topic) Source 1 (Bibliography)

Approximately 250 million children between the ages of 5 and 14 work in developing countries in Asia, Africa, and Latin America. Almost half of them—120 million—work on a full-time basis in industries ranging from agriculture to manufacturing. (Summary)

p. 25

Note: Well-known human rights organization
Possible use: Introduction

ZIP TIPS

The topics and subtopics on your note cards will form the main or body paragraphs in your paper.

Here's a stinker:

Child Labor	Not-for-profit organization publication

Many underdeveloped countries use child labor in all facets of work—
agriculture, manufacturing, trade, and services. Advocates say that
such child labor is exploitative and places children at great risk because
of unhealthy work conditions, their inability to access education, and low
wages. Agencies that are trying to remedy the situation include UNICEF,
International Labor Organization, and Human Rights Watch.

What makes the first note card a good one?

- It has a label that shows its topic or subtopic, which reflects the main idea of the card.

- There's a library call number so you can locate the book again.

- There is a notation about the source, keyed to your bibliography, so you know from what text the note came.

- You've been smart enough to include the page number (if available).

- There isn't too much information on the card. One fact, summary statement, paraphrase, or quotation per card is a good rule of thumb.

- You've added a note to jog your memory about why this note is important and possibly where it might fit in your paper.

- You've noted whether you've paraphrased or summarized the source or if it's a direct quotation.

And why is the second card a stinker?

- The second card's information only lists a very general topic, has no specific source citation to relate it to a bibliographic reference, has an incomplete source reference that doesn't tell where the information can be found, has more than one idea on the card (and that information is not precise), does not include a source page number, and has no additional notes that might be helpful later on.

Go Electronic

If the thought of writing anything longhand makes your fingers cramp, take notes on your computer. When working with printed material, first mark the passages or information that you may want to record on a note card. Then, go back and type that information onto a separate page just like an index card. You can file similar information by subject and also have everything from separate sources easy to locate. If you're working from a Web page, you can, of course, cut and paste materials, but be sure that you put quotations marks around information you take word-for-word, or that ugly plagiarism will pop up again.

WHAT TO WRITE

When taking notes, you don't want to rewrite the entire article or book on note cards. You want to extract the supporting information that is relevant to your topic, analysis, or argument. Reading and continuing to evaluate the material you've gathered are your first steps in taking good notes. If you try to take notes before you've absorbed or evaluated the material, you'll only be creating more work for yourself.

Give yourself a break while reading and evaluating the material by taking some shortcuts. In a book, scan the table of contents and

ZIP TIPS

Put one thought, fact, summary statement, paraphrase, or quotation per note card. Be sure to use quotation marks on your note card for anything that you copy word-for-word from a book, Web site, or other source. Then, when you write your paper, you'll immediately know it's someone else's words or ideas and that a citation needs to be made.

index to see if there's information on your topic (try some synonyms also). Read the author's preface, introductory chapter, and conclusion and also look at the sources cited to get a good sense about content, the arguments being presented, and some leads for more research. You may find that a book or article from your preliminary research really isn't on target for your paper. If so, skip the notes.

As you read, look for juicy quotes, statistics, supporting and opposing opinions, explanations, and general information to frame your argument or analysis. Make sure the material is from reliable sources and will support your position or analysis. You want the important stuff. Even then you'll probably take more notes than you need, but you'll weed out what you don't want when you start putting your paper together.

ZIP TIPS

If you know how to use a database, such as Microsoft Access, it's another way to create your bibliography and track and sort your sources. If you don't, forget it. You could spend more time learning the software than it takes to research and write your paper.

Don't rely too much on a single source. Mix it up with books, periodicals, electronic sources, and audiovisual materials as appropriate. Using only one main source makes your research paper look like a fifth grader's first stab at writing a paper. You may find some sources have richer material and generate more note cards, but try to balance them out.

Write your notes carefully. When making notes, you'll be jotting down ideas and content in your own shorthand–so be sure you can read it. You will also usually be either recording direct quotes, summarizing information, or paraphrasing information, that is, rewriting the author's original words in your own. This can be tricky, so take your time and be precise.

Direct Quotations

With direct quotations, you must copy the words exactly, even if there are mistakes, such as spelling or factual errors, and put them in quotation marks. Highlight them, circle them, or draw attention to them in some way so you know they are quotes. If there is an error in the quotation, include it. You can always mark the error with the word [*sic*], which means "as written," next to the mistake. In this original statement, for example, "Terorism has grown to be a world-wide phenomenon," the word "terorism" is misspelled. Your direct quotation note should read, "Terorism [*sic*] has grown to be a world-wide phenomenon."

If you skip some parts of the quotation, use an **ellipsis,** a set of three spaced dots that indicates words have been omitted. If a word or phrase is omitted at the end of a sentence, use four spaced dots.

For instance, the original quote may read:

"Tsunami is a set of ocean waves caused by any large, abrupt disturbance of the sea-surface. If the disturbance is close to the coastline, local tsunamis can demolish coastal communities within minutes. A very large disturbance can cause local devastation AND export tsunami destruction thousands of miles away. The word tsunami is a Japanese word, represented by two characters: tsu, meaning, "harbor", and nami meaning, "wave". Tsunamis rank high on the scale of natural disasters. Since 1850 alone, tsunamis have been responsible for the loss of over 420,000 lives and billions of dollars of damage to coastal structures and habitats. Most of these casualties were caused by local tsunamis that occur about once per year somewhere in the world. For example, the December 26, 2004, tsunami killed about 130,000 people close to the earthquake and about 58,000 people on distant shores. Predicting when and where the next tsunami will strike is currently impossible. Once the tsunami is generated, forecasting tsunami arrival and impact is possible through modeling and measurement technologies." (Source: Bernard, Eddie N. "The Tsunami Story." Available from www.tsunami.noaa.gov/tsunami_story.html, accessed 07 February 2007).

You may want to omit a significant portion of the information in which case you would show the quotation as follows:

"Tsunami is a set of ocean waves caused by any large, abrupt disturbance of the sea-surface. If the disturbance is close to the coastline, local tsunamis can demolish coastal communities within minutes. A very large disturbance can cause local devastation AND

export tsunami destruction thousands of miles away . . . Predicting when and where the next tsunami will strike is currently impossible. Once the tsunami is generated, forecasting tsunami arrival and impact is possible through modeling and measurement technologies." (Source: Bernard, Eddie N. "The Tsunami Story." Available from www.tsunami.noaa.gov/tsunami_story.html, accessed 07 February 2007).

Summaries

A **summary** focuses on key ideas and supporting evidence from the source without writing down every piece of detailed information. It's a condensed version of the original information and is usually about one quarter the length of the original quote.

A summary of the original quotation about the tsunami might read:

Since 1850, tsunamis, one of the world's most destructive natural disasters, have killed 420,000 people and caused billions of dollars of damage. Arising from sudden and large disruptions at the ocean's surface, tsunamis can wipe out local coastal communities in minutes and spread destruction for thousands of miles. Current modeling and measurement technologies only allow us to chart tsunamis' impact, rather than to predict their occurrence. (Source: Bernard, Eddie N. "The Tsunami Story." Available from www.tsunami. noaa.gov/tsunami_story.html, accessed 07 February 2007)

Paraphrasing

Another method of making a note, paraphrasing can be tricky as you are basically rewriting the author's original words in your own words. You have to read and understand the original passage in order to restate the material *in your own words*. The paraphrase is usually almost as long as the original passage and contains the same ideas in the same order as the original.

A paraphrase of our direct quotation might read:

Tsunamis are some of the world's most devastating natural disasters, especially for coastal communities in their paths. Their name, from the Japanese words for harbor (tsu) and wave (nami), reflects their nature: sudden disruptions of the sea at its surface resulting in a set of ocean waves. Since 1850, coastal area tsunamis have caused over 420,000 deaths, as well as extensive and costly damage to man-made and natural environments. Damage from tsunamis occurs locally, yet extends far beyond the center of the disaster. On December 26, 2004, 130,000 people in the immediate area of a tsunami lost their lives; another 58,000 living miles away also died. Ironically, most recorded losses have been the result of just one local tsunami each year in some area of the world. Although tsunamis can be tracked once they occur, there are still no accurate methods of predicting their occurrence or foretelling their arrival. (Source: Bernard, Eddie N. "The Tsunami Story." Available from www.tsunami.noaa.gov/tsunami_story.html, accessed 07 February 2007)

TOO MUCH OR TOO LITTLE

Remember that writing a research paper is a process and that you'll be making adjustments along the way. Take stock of what you've got early so that if you need to go back to the library and gather more sources or diversify your sources, it won't be right before your paper is due. You don't want to sit down to begin to write and find that you've got gaping information holes the size of the Grand Canyon.

Pump It Up

If your topic and thesis are too narrow and you simply can't find enough material to back up your argument that one well-known hamburger chain really does have better French fries than the other, bump the topic up a notch to the next level of generality. Focusing on the marketing techniques of one or two fast-food chains and how they carve out a market niche might prove to be a winner in the source competition.

Focus In

You can narrow down your topic by applying some limiters to your topic: Who? What? When? and Where? Can you specify a particular era or time period, such as the social importance of comics in the 1950s? A smaller piece of the pie, such as anorexic teenage males instead of anorexic teenagers? One or two particularly interesting persons, events, or institutions instead of three to five? A more limited geographic location? For example, a paper on HIV/AIDS in Botswana might be easier to manage than HIV/AIDS in Africa.

Stay Flexible

As you do your research, you will probably find new information that may cause you to rethink your proposed thesis, that argues against your position, or that totally causes you to rethink your research question. Keep an open mind and keep track of these thoughts on a separate page or in a separate file from your source notes.

UNZIPPING RIGHT ALONG

- Put a system in place to help you track your research.

- Write your notes legibly, or type them so they make sense, without too many obscure abbreviations. Otherwise, you may not be able to interpret them correctly later on.

- Consult the appropriate style manual (as required or preferred by your instructor) before beginning your bibliography or note cards.

- Be selective about your sources. Not all sources will be relevant even if you initially thought they were. Not every fact, opinion, or explanation will be worth a note card. Only use items relevant to your analysis or argument.

- Keep an open mind about your topic. Remember, not enough available resources—or too many—may mean you have to either narrow or broaden your topic.

HIDDEN SNAGS

- Not doing enough research to diversify your sources. One book, even if it's the "go-to" book for the subject, isn't enough to make your paper a research paper.

- Forgetting to put quotations around direct quotations. By the time you've plowed through a ton of research materials, you won't remember whether or not something is a direct quotation.

- Not checking your note cards for completeness and accuracy BEFORE you put away your source material, return that book to the library, or zap your source into cyberspace.

MORE TO UNZIP

Sloppy note-taking breeds sloppy thinking and hampers your ability to organize your paper. If you don't want to be frantically looking for that one critical piece of information, find a way to neaten up.

Note cards for bibliographic sources and source notes are a tried-and-true way to tackle the organization issue. Notes also help you stay focused on your topic and develop or refine your thesis. Read first, write second for the best notes. If the handwritten note style isn't for you, find a way to incorporate the concepts into an electronic tracking method.

Following the style manual preferred or assigned by your instructor from the start will save you time later in doing your bibliography, footnotes, endnotes, and other pesky, but necessary, details. If in doubt about what style to use, ask your instructor!

HOOK ME UP TO MORE RESOURCES

- *Research Papers for Dummies* by Geraldine Woods. Hoboken: Wiley Publishing, Inc., 2002, has an in-depth chapter on making the most of your note-taking and how to avoid making mistakes when you do.

- Check out "Researching and Organizing Your Paper: The Note Card System" at **http://depts.gallaudet.edu/ englishworks/writing/notecard.html.** This site will also link you to handouts on the MLA, APA, and Chicago style of citations.

- The Purdue Writer's Workshop at **http://owl.english. purdue.edu** has some good advice about how to broaden or narrow your topic.

CHAPTER 5

Fitting the Pieces Together:
Analyze & Organize Some More

YOU'RE PROBABLY WONDERING: Am I ever actually going to write this paper? Yes, you eventually will, but not yet. You still need to continue to analyze and organize your information into an outline or another graphic form.

Why? By setting down your ideas in an orderly fashion, seeing where your research fits in (and where you might need some more information), and testing your main point, you'll start to see how the paper will flow and how you'll want to fill in the details to support your ideas in each section. Writing it should then be a snap! Okay, maybe not a snap, but at least a lot easier.

This chapter reveals:

- Methods to Structure Your Paper

- Ways to Sort Out Your Info

- Ways to Refine Your Main Point and Fill in the Facts

WHY BOTHER?

The **outline** can help you overcome one of the hardest parts of doing a research paper: starting the writing process.

How? An outline gives you an initial structure to start to organize your main ideas and fill them in with specific supporting evidence and ideas gleaned from your research. It gives you a good visual reference to help you quickly see what's working and what isn't and where you have gaps in your research.

Your outline is a map that will help you get to your destination—a finished paper—more quickly. If you start on a trip without a map and you only have a vague idea of how to reach your destination, it will probably take you longer to get to there. If you've got an unlimited amount of time to reach your destination, great. You don't need a map. But, with a research paper, you've certainly got a deadline to meet. With an outline to organize your thoughts and your research, you might take some detours, but you've improved your chances of achieving your goal of submitting a well-organized research paper on time.

ZIP TIPS

Some instructors require students to submit a well-developed outline as part of the assignment. Be sure to check, as you don't want to skip an important part of the research paper assignment!

Remember the advice to make it bite-sized? By grouping your main and subordinate ideas together logically in an outline, you can begin to attack your writing bit by bit. Once you've got the structure or the bare bones of your paper, if you get stuck, you can move onto another section and then return to that more difficult section later.

WHEN DO I MAKE AN OUTLINE?

There isn't a set rule. If you know your topic well, you can probably zip off a brief outline right at the start of your research paper. If, however, you're unsure of your subject matter, the direction your paper will take, or the availability of information on the topic, don't stress yourself out trying to construct an outline before doing some research.

In any event, you'll find it will be easier to construct a more detailed outline as you get a better grip on your topic and thesis. Remember also that your outline will change over time as you gather more information and start to organize your notes, so don't regard it as something set in stone.

WHAT'S IN AN OUTLINE?

Your outline will be divided into three main parts, just like your finished paper:

1. Introduction

2. Body of the paper

3. Conclusion

The **introduction** should include your thesis statement and some background information about the topic of your paper. The **body** will be subdivided into major sections that correspond to the main arguments or points you want to make. Each major section can be further subdivided into subtopics with your supporting evidence. These main sections and subsections will correspond to paragraphs in the paper. The **conclusion** will be your opportunity to zip everything together.

A **topical outline** will state the major subject headings as nouns or a phrase. A **sentence outline** will include full sentences, as you might expect. By writing complete sentences, you'll have a head start on writing your paper. Just be consistent—either use topics or sentences, but don't mix them in the same outline.

ZIP TIPS

Don't let an outline drive your research or cause you to overlook some interesting or important aspect of your topic simply because you didn't think to include it in your outline. Always keep an open mind.

The Working Outline

You can get started on making a **working outline** by simply listing some of the questions that you already have, or are thinking about, as you do your research. The working outline helps you identify some of the major topics you think you'll address in your paper. As you do more research and focus in on your topic and main point, you may find that some of these ideas continue to fit right in; others you may find are no longer relevant.

For example, after some research for a paper on eating disorders among female athletes in college, your initial outline might develop from these questions:

- What is the prevalence of eating disorders among female athletes in college?

- What are the risk factors for athletes who develop eating disorders?

ZIP TIPS

Outlines are a great way to get some feedback from your instructor or classmates about your project. They don't have to slog through the whole document, and you'll get some constructive ideas before you start writing.

- Who is responsible for athletes' health and well-being?

- Why do eating disorders go unidentified?

- What pressures do coaches put on their athletes that lead to eating disorders?

- Why don't coaches do more to identify and resolve the problem?

So here is our initial outline:

I. Statistics on eating disorders: What is the prevalence of eating disorders among female athletes in college?

II. Risk Factors: What are the risk factors for athletes who develop eating disorders?

III. Role of Coach: Who is responsible for athletes' health and well-being?

IV. Pressures to win versus healthy athletes: What pressures do coaches put on their athletes that lead to eating disorders or cause them to persist?

V. Knowledge about eating disorders: Why don't coaches do more to identify and resolve the problem?

VI. Failure to intervene: Why don't coaches do more to get athletes help?

As you read more, you'll begin to develop subtopics and points under each category. You may even add new subtopics and points. You can use this outline as a starting point and reorganize it as your research and thesis develop.

The Zipped Up Formal Outline

You probably learned how to write an outline in elementary school with those clunky Roman numerals. Guess what? The format for a typical formal outline still has the same structure and those Roman numerals. You can fill it in as a topical or sentence outline. This is the outline style that you might be asked to use if your instructor requires you to submit an outline as an interim step in writing your paper.

I. Introduction
II. Main topic
  A. Subtopic
    1. Main point
      a.
        i.
        ii.
      b.
        i.
        ii.
    2. Main point
      a.
        i.
        ii.
      b.
        i.
        ii.
  B. Subtopic
    1. Main point
      a.
        i.
        ii.

     b.
      i.
      ii.
    2. Main point
     a.
      i.
      ii.
     b.
      i.
      ii.

III, IV, V, and so on with their subdivisions to the conclusion, which also receives a Roman numeral. You can subdivide the subdivisions ad infinitum, but don't go overboard.

The Unzipped Informal Outline

The previous format is a good guide for constructing a classic outline, but it's not the only way to write an outline. If Roman numerals aren't your thing, use regular numbers to label major sections. Or skip the numbers and just make major headings and add bullets underneath for your major points and subpoints. For example:

   Introduction

    Background Information

    Thesis Statement

  First Subtopic

    Main Argument or Point 1

      • Supporting Evidence

      • Supporting Evidence

Main Argument or Point 2

- Supporting Evidence
- Supporting Evidence

Second Subtopic

Main Argument or Point 1

- Supporting Evidence
- Supporting Evidence

Main Argument or Point 2

- Supporting Evidence
- Supporting Evidence

Third Subtopic

Main Argument or Point 1

- Supporting Evidence
- Supporting Evidence

Main Argument or Point 2

- Supporting Evidence
- Supporting Evidence

Conclusion

SAMPLE OUTLINE

The following outline is an example of a formal topical outline using Roman numerals. As noted, it won't pop out of your head in this complete form. It develops as you read and research your subject matter. You'll fill in main points and subpoints as you go along and maybe even change the order of the outline.

Title: *Pushing to the Limit:*
College Coaches as a Risk Factor in
Eating Disorders among Female Athletes

I. Introduction
    A. Quotation, statistic, or example about eating disorders among female college athletes
    B. Background about eating disorders
        1. Prevalence
        2. Causes
        3. Reasons for concern
    C. Thesis Statement—*Although they should be the first line of defense in preventing eating disorders, college coaches are themselves a risk factor in the development and perpetuation of these illnesses among female athletes.*

II. Focus on results
    A. Emphasis on performance
        1. Low body fat and performance
        2. Optimum weight and performance

   B. Emphasis on winning
      1. Winning as only focus
      2. Importance of team over individual athlete

III. Stress on weight and looks
   A. Weight-control techniques
      1. Weigh-ins
      2. Restrictive eating

ZIP TIPS

As you develop your outline, remember these important features:

- Outlines organize information in a hierarchy and cover the entire scope of your paper.

- Outlines go from the general to the specific. A major heading states a general topic, and each subheading states more specific information.

- Major sections of outlines should be equal in importance in terms of the information they contain.

- Outlines are parallel in structure. If you use a noun as a first heading, the other headings are nouns also. Don't mix nouns, verbs, and sentences.

- Each section needs at least two parts; you can't have I without II, A without B, A1 without A2, or A.1.a without A.2.a.

    B. Coaches' personal views about weight and body image
1. Personal preferences for thinness
2. Validation and respect for thinness
3. Impact of casual comments about weight

IV. Lack of knowledge about eating disorders
    A. Inadequate education about eating disorders
    B. Lack of understanding about causes of eating disorders
    C. Failure to recognize symptoms and signs

V. Reluctance to intervene
    A. Responsibility of individual
    B. Responsibility of family members
    C. Responsibility of other professionals
    D. Lack of confidence in dealing with eating disorders

VI. Conclusion
    A. Coach as risk factor
    B. Mandatory training of coaches
    C. Need for better college/university policies

MAP IT? CUBE IT? OTHER WAYS TO GET IT TOGETHER

Informal and formal outlines are the classic ways to get a grip on your research and to kick start your writing process. If they don't work for you, drawing a graphic can help you get a visual image of your paper and see how its parts might start to fit together.

You might, for example, draw a **pyramid** starting with your thesis or research question at the top and the elements of your main points in the layers below. All ideas lead to the apex of the pyramid. Like an outline, the pyramid is a hierarchical ordering.

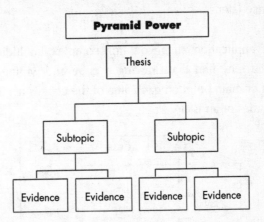

Or, you might use a technique (which is also useful for brainstorming) called **mapping** or **clustering.** It's simple. Put your central idea in the middle of a circle and then draw lines out from

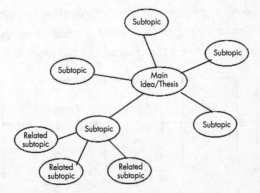

it to other circles that contain topics related to the main idea. Each circle can then have a series of sub-circles with topics related to that circle. You'll easily see the major categories of your paper, although they won't necessarily be in order. You can then put them in sequence later.

If a 3-D application suits you (for complex, multidimensional ideas), you may find that drawing a **cube** and writing down an argument or main point on each face of the cube is a good way to view all sides of an issue.

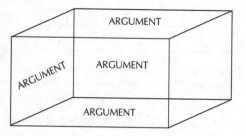

Flow charts are especially good ways to represent research papers that focus on a process, as you're focusing on the logical progression of one idea from another through a series of boxes linked by arrows showing the direction of the process.

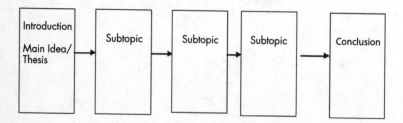

DIVIDE AND CONQUER

Sort It Out

Assuming you've made and labeled some kind of note card, simply sort the cards with similar topics or subtopics into piles as a first step in organizing the scads of notes you've taken. You'll have a pile for each topic or subtopic and can judge if you have enough evidence to make your case or analysis. You'll also be able to see easily if you have drawn on a diversity of source types—books, periodicals, and electronic sources—especially ones that might be required by your instructor. These piles can even be the start of a working outline if you don't already have one.

If you started off with a well-focused idea, immediately drew up a working outline, and were super organized taking notes, you might even have your notes already categorized and labeled by the subtopics of your working outline. In that case, congratulations! You're way ahead of the game. Most students, though, have to sort and re-sort, focus and refocus, review and refine before nailing everything into place. That's normal, so don't worry.

Re-sort and Regroup

If you do a first sort and come up with 100 different categories of notes, you've probably labeled each note card with a different topic. Reexamine the cards, and think about how those topics or subtopics relate to each other. Then relabel/regroup your note cards into a more manageable number of categories. Some notes may fall into more than one category. Make copies and put them in both piles. As you work through your outline, you'll see where they fit in most logically.

For that paper on eating disorders, for example, you may find that your notes fall into these piles of information:

- National Collegiate Athletic Association (NCAA) statistics on eating disorders

- American Journal of College Health statistics on eating disorders

- Case studies of eating disorders

- The Telltale Signs: Female Athlete Triad

- Anorexia (definition)

- Bulimia (definition)

- Symptoms and signs of eating disorders

- Misinformation about body image and weight

- Prescreening high school recruits

- Training about eating disorders

- Emotional and psychological stresses

- Preventative measures

- Pressure to win

- Guidelines for coaches

If you re-sort the notes, you can whittle these categories down to:

- Statistics about eating disorders (NCAA, American Journal of College Health stats)

- Symptoms and signs of eating disorders (Female Athlete Triad)

- Types of eating disorders (anorexia, bulimia, others)

- Risk factors (misinformation about body image/weight, emotional and psychological stresses, pressure to win)

- Preventative measures (prescreening, training, guidelines for coaches)

- Case studies of eating disorders

If you've really focused on the main point of your paper while you've done your research, each topic or subtopic will fit into the analysis or argument and become either a main paragraph or some part of a supporting paragraph in your paper. You may also find that some of the information or notes aren't really useful in helping you make your analysis or argument. Set them aside, but don't throw them out; if you shift your topic or main point slightly you might need them after all.

TEST DRIVE YOUR THESIS STATEMENT

As you organize and analyze your notes and write your outline, your thesis statement will become clearer to you. Remember, even if you are asked to provide an analysis rather than make a persuasive argument, you still need to make a claim or have a main point and be able to support it. Summarizing your reading isn't enough!

It's Getting Clearer

Believe it or not, you will see a pattern of information emerge as you review your notes. Sometimes, that pattern might surprise you and may even cause you to rethink the original direction or main point of your paper.

For example, while conducting research on eating disorders among female college athletes, you begin to realize that there is a lot of available information about this topic. Perhaps your initial thought was to concentrate on the athletes themselves. Based on your reading, however, you ask yourself: Why do these patterns of eating disorders still persist when they are a well-documented problem for female athletes? You read a lot about risk factors—the competitive environment, emphasis on the perfect weight and body for particular sports, and so on. Your reading leads you to understand that the coach bears a lot of responsibility for creating the standards and environment in which these athletes compete. You come up with the idea that perhaps the coaches themselves are a risk factor in the development and persistence of eating disorders among female athletes in college.

Your reading could lead you to the opposite, equally defensible, position that because coaches develop a close relationship with their athletes, they are the key factor in the prevention and treatment of eating disorders among female athletes, rather than one of the risk factors. Whichever position you decide to adopt, the important point is that you have identified an arguable thesis for this persuasive paper that can be supported by the material you have researched.

Make the Connection

Once you get your outline together, test drive your thesis another way by writing out topic sentences and seeing how they relate to your thesis. If you can't make a logical connection, you may need to rework your thesis or reconsider your line of argument or analysis. Let's look again at our outline for our paper on eating disorders.

Introduction: Background information on eating disorders among female athletes.

Thesis: Although they should be the first line of defense in preventing eating disorders, college coaches are themselves a risk factor in the development and perpetuation of these illnesses among female athletes.

First main topic: Coaches overlook eating disorders because they are focused on training their athletes to compete and win.

- *How it zips up with the thesis:* For coaches, the health and well-being of the athletes are secondary to winning and optimum performance.

Second main topic: Coaches' emphasis on weight and looks pressures female athletes to lose weight by any means.

- *How it zips up with the thesis:* Athletes get the message that controlling weight and conforming to their coaches' ideas about ideal body image are critical even if they lead to unhealthy eating patterns.

Third main topic: Coaches lack knowledge and understanding about eating disorders.

- *How it zips up with the thesis:* Eating disorders go undetected and unidentified because coaches do not recognize their physical symptoms and emotional signs.

Fourth main topic: Coaches do not perceive confronting athletes about eating disorders to be their responsibility and fail to intervene.

- *How it zips up with the thesis:* Coaches can't be part of the solution if they don't think it's their job.

FILLING IN THE FACTS: HOW YOUR RESEARCH FITS IN

Support Your Point of View

So you've sketched out your main idea and a preliminary order for discussing your main points. Here's where you'll start to figure out exactly where your notes will fit into your outline as supporting evidence. What's the supporting evidence? All those examples, quotations, citations from experts, personal interviews, summaries, and paraphrases that you've amassed are supporting evidence that back up your ideas and analysis. What else does it back up? All those brilliant thoughts that you also remembered to jot down as you took notes on your sources.

As your outline becomes more specific and detailed, you can start plugging in your evidence into specific places in the outline. By doing this, you'll see if you have enough evidence or if you need to do some more research to back up what you say. If all the evidence comes from one source, you obviously need to find more sources. Two or three pieces of evidence to back up your statements in each major paragraph of your paper are usually sufficient to support your point.

ZIP TIPS

For a reality check, before you get too attached, read the main point or thesis of your paper to a friend to see if it makes sense to someone other than you.

Organize the Evidence

The way that your research fits into your paper depends on how you decide to organize your materials to support your thesis or main point. The assignment directions may give you a strong clue about a logical way to organize your paper, especially if the words "compare and contrast" or "argue" are involved.

There's no right way to organize your information, but information in one section of your outline needs to flow logically into another. Typical ways to organize your overall paper (and also paragraphs within the paper) are:

Chronological Order

Here you are developing and tracing a timeline of events or a process that occurs over time. Look for major timeframes or

ZIP TIPS

Each piece of evidence has a job: to develop your argument or analysis. If it doesn't, replace it with a piece that does.

milestones as ways to subdivide your paper into topics or subtopics. For a paper on the early days of the Civil Rights Movement in the l950s and 1960s, turning points such as Rosa Parks' famous bus ride, Brown v. Board of Education, and Martin Luther King's assassination could be organized and discussed in chronological order. Or, for a longer paper, you might look at the civil rights issue by decades: the 1930s, 1940s, and 1950s.

Categories or Classification

Here information, examples, or evidence is arranged by subject matter. For example, you might divide your paper about the Civil Rights Movement into categories such as history, economics, and politics of the movement.

Compare and Contrast

This is often a typical assignment from an instructor that asks you to arrange information by similarities or differences. For example: Compare and contrast Jane Austen and Emily Brontë's views of women's social roles in their novels.

Order of Importance

Here you arrange your points by paragraph so that you are leading up from the least important point (paragraph) to your most important point (paragraph) in the paper. You're building momentum throughout the paper up to the major point that clinches your argument or analysis.

Cause and Effect

This is a tricky one because you want to be sure that a cause-and-effect relationship truly exists. To say that the former Soviet Union collapsed because people were tired of not having access to fast food might be a stretch, but you should be able to draw a logical thread between economic conditions and the fall of the Soviet Union.

Pro and Con

This is a typical structure for an argumentative research paper. You to present both sides of the argument—the opposition's side and your side, plus the evidence that supports your argument.

UNZIPPING RIGHT ALONG

- Review and analyze your notes thoroughly so that you can pinpoint what it is you want to say in your thesis statement.

- Understand that nothing is yet set in stone; your thesis may change as you review your materials, and your outline might also shift considerably.

- Keep all versions and drafts of your outline and thesis so that you can take what's good and use it in your next version, rather than starting all over again.

- Use your outline as a guide to help you check if your thesis works and if you've got enough specific evidence to support your analysis or argument.

HIDDEN SNAGS

- Beginning to write your paper before you've tried to develop an outline or some map of your ideas based on your research and notes.

- Spending more time perfecting the format of your outline than filling it in with ideas and supporting evidence.

MORE TO UNZIP

The buildup to writing your research paper is as important as the actual writing. In fact, many instructors consider this phase to be critical to writing an excellent paper. Once they read your paper, they'll know immediately if you've put time and effort on the prep work: thinking about how to present your material and laying out a logical sequence of information and evidence.

Some instructors will even help you as you try to conquer the techniques of writing a research paper by requesting an outline of your paper for critique before you hand in the final product. They don't want you to flop any more than you do. So, you can either present a disorganized mess that rambles on and fades into a less-than-inspiring conclusion, or wow and zow them with a sparkling gem of well-organized thoughts backed up by the power of your well-researched evidence. It's your choice!

- Trying to make a round peg fit into a square hole. If your notes on a particular topic or subtopic turn out to be irrelevant to making your main point, don't include them!

- Failing to go back to your sources (or the library if need be) when your outline is screaming that more evidence is needed to back up your claim.

HOOK ME UP TO MORE RESOURCES

- To learn more about making a graphic of your research paper and refining your thesis, check out the University of Richmond Writing Center, which is also a great overall resource for writing your paper, at **http://writing2. richmond.edu/writing/wweb.html.**

- Need some more alternatives to the outline? Check out Paradigm Online Writing Assistant at **http://my.powa.org.**

- Several online sources offer templates that can help you structure your outline for an analytical or argumentative paper. Check out: **http://owl.english. purdue.edu/workshops/hypertext/ResearchW/outline. html** or **http://www.rio.maricopa.edu/distance_learning/ tutorials/writing_guide/create_a_paper.shtml.**

CHAPTER 6

**Unzipping Your First Draft:
Pulling It Together, Writing,
and Revising**

FINALLY! YOU CAN sit down and do some serious writing. By now, you've done a lot of the hard work: chosen a topic, gotten a specific focus and main point or thesis, searched every nook and cranny for material to back up your main point, organized your notes, and mapped out a preliminary structure for your research paper. That blank piece of paper may still look awfully blank, but you have a good grasp of what you want to say.

At this point, your biggest problem will probably be that your mind seems to be frozen in a mental glacier of writer's block or that you're hyperventilating into a brown paper bag trying to avoid a panic attack.

This chapter reveals how to:

- Set a Tone and Style

- Understand the Main Parts of the Research Paper

- Make the Best Use of Your Research

- Avoid Writer's Block and Panic Attacks

ARE YOU TALKIN' TO ME? YOUR AUDIENCE

"Audience? What audience?" you're asking yourself. Even if you're not presenting your paper in front of the class, you still have an audience: your readers. You're thinking about them consciously or unconsciously as you progress from floundering around for a topic to putting pen to paper (or fingers to the keyboard) to write your first draft. After all, isn't the first question you ask yourself: "What does my instructor want?" Right there, you're thinking about your audience. If you're writing a senior thesis for high school or college, you will probably have more than one audience member, as a committee usually reviews theses.

Your job as the writer is to present your material in a compelling, readable, and clear way. Don't assume that someone knows all the terms or concepts you use in your paper, but don't over-explain either. If you're writing mainly for your instructor, you can assume that he or she knows the terminology associated with his or her subject area. If you're writing for a thesis committee with instructors from various disciplines, you may need a few more definitions or additional explanations.

STYLE AND TONE

Even though your research paper is an academic paper, it doesn't have to be *BORING.* Consider the plight of your instructor who has to read hundreds of research papers. Sure, it's his or her job, but give your instructor a break and inject some thought into your writing.

Style

Style refers to your particular way of writing; it's an important part of how you present yourself and your thoughts. Academic writing doesn't have to be as dry as dust or as stiff as a board, but you also don't want to swing too far in the direction of slang or everyday spoken language.

Unless you're writing a paper about the use of slang as a cultural unifying force among teenagers, opening your paper with "Hey, Dude!" or "Hey, Babe!" and sprinkling slang expressions throughout isn't going to cut it. On the other hand, you also don't want to sound like some pompous, stuffy academic who uses long words and even longer sentences in an attempt to bowl over the audience with his or her brilliance. Leave that to the professionals. You'll only sound ridiculous, and your audience won't know or care what you're talking about. Use words you know and understand.

You can make your writing interesting and creative by following these tips:

- Punch up your vocabulary. Don't use the same words over and over again. Check your thesaurus or dictionary and find a synonym!

- Use the active, rather than passive, voice—that is, interject some motion and action into your sentences by allowing your subjects to do something. "The dog bit Bob's hand" (active voice) is a lot more interesting than "Bob's hand was bitten by the dog."

- Show rather than tell. "The penguins dive into the cold water" tells the reader about the temperature of the water, but "The penguins propel themselves off the rocks into the icy waters below" sets a scene in the reader's mind.

- Vary your sentence structure. If every sentence starts the same way or follows the same structure, you've already bored your reader to tears. Mix up simple sentences with longer complex sentences. Instead of writing "She went to the library. She sat down at the computer. She started typing her paper," string the sentences together: "She went to the library where she sat down at the computer and began to type her paper."

- Avoid clichés and tired phrases, such as "It goes without saying," "History tells us," or "In my humble opinion." You won't fool anyone; your own opinion is never humble.

- Eliminate redundancies such as *past experience, close proximity,* and *end result.*

- Interject some humor, but only if it's appropriate.

Tone

You may be passionate about a subject or your point of view, but don't go overboard in how you state your case. You don't want your readers to feel as though you are lecturing them or that you are so opinionated or angry that you're unbearable. Be sure to use language that is gender-neutral and respectful of physical differences, age, race, and ethnicity.

CRAFTING THE TITLE, INTRODUCTION, BODY, AND CONCLUSION

Research papers follow a set order

1. Title

2. Introduction

3. Body

4. Conclusion

Every part should relate to your main point. Each part should also be connected in some way to the part that precedes it and follows it. The point is to have an integrated whole, whose parts fit together like a jigsaw puzzle, with each piece adding something important to developing the overall picture.

ZIP TIPS

Save those catchy abbreviations that you use in text messages and e-mails, such as IMHO, OTOH, and FYI, for cyberspace. They don't belong in your research paper.

Title

The title might be the last item you write, but it will be the first item that your reader sees. It should reveal your topic in a short, zippy way and not ramble on so that your audience is drifting off before they've even turned past the title page.

Which one sounds more interesting? "The Media and Its Role in the Promotion of Thinness as a Culturally Desirable Body Form for Teenagers" or "The Media and the Adolescent Cult of Thinness?" Both get the point across, but the latter invites the reader to find out more.

Introduction

Your introduction will give your reader several important pieces of information: a bit of background information, your topic, your thesis or research question, and your line of argument or analysis. It provides a frame of reference for your reader and sets the tone for the rest of your paper.

In the introduction, you not only want to inform your reader about what's coming up, but you also want to catch your reader's attention. Your introduction is like a job interview. First impressions are the lasting ones, and you only have a few seconds to make a good first impression.

"This paper analyzes the role of global warming in the eradication of the habitat of the Emperor penguin" is a ho-hum opening sentence. It's less likely to draw the reader in than a bold statement of fact (but make sure it's factual; this one is made up) such as: *"Recent*

research on global warming shows that the Emperor penguins' Ant-arctic habitat has been reduced to a 1-square-mile ice floe."

Consider opening with a quotation from an expert: *"The fossil record conclusively shows that 50-ton turtles roamed across North American 100,000 years ago," says noted paleontologist Danielle Bonehunter.*

Short anecdotes can be eye-openers and introduce your topic in an unusual way. For example, *"Stephanie arrived at college as an accomplished high school track star with an impressive array of medals and trophies. She seemed to be the picture of health. Within three months, she had lost 30 pounds and was hospitalized and let go from the team."* Readers will want to find out more about the cause of Stephanie's problem and the topic of your paper: eating disorders among female college athletes.

ZIP TIPS

Your instructor already knows what the assignment is so don't repeat it word for word in the introduction.

Other starter options are a question, an ironic statement, or an opinion that is contrary to the one that you are going to argue. There are lots of possibilities; just find one that's interesting to you and that you think will hook your readers.

To add to that startling statement about penguins, a more complete introduction could read: *"Research on global warming shows that the Emperor penguins' Antarctic habitat has been reduced to a 1-square-mile ice floe and that their source of food has been severely diminished. Unable to adjust to these new environmental circumstances, the penguins have voluntarily relocated to a zoo in suburban Buenos Aires where their quality of life has vastly improved. Despite arguments to the contrary, global warming can and does have unexpected positive consequences for some species."* Now you've got your readers' attention and have stated your thesis and announced your topic and line of argument.

ZIP TIPS

Write your thesis statement down, but leave writing the introduction until last. It's often the hardest section to write. Don't get writer's block right at the start!

Body

The body of the paper will offer your main points and subpoints, your evidence, and supporting arguments that drive to your conclusion. Each paragraph presents another piece of the puzzle. They should all zip together neatly to make the whole.

In the body of the paper, you can offer an explanation, compare and contrast various viewpoints and arguments, offer a solution, provide evidence, and present facts. The way in which you order your information will depend on the assignment and how you can make best use of your information.

If you look at your outline, each major section should form a paragraph with one main idea. Each paragraph should have a similar structure to your overall paper: an introduction through a topic sentence, a body with facts, arguments, examples, and so on, and a concluding sentence. Because you are presenting an important point in each paragraph, each paragraph should be about the same length.

Use transition words or phrases to keep the ideas flowing within and between paragraphs. They'll make your sentences more interesting and will lead your reader easily from one idea to the next. Examples of transition words and phrases that can be used to link related ideas are:

- Also

- Although

- Consequently

- However

- Thus

- In fact

- As a result

- In addition

- On the one hand

- On the other hand

- Specifically

Conclusion

Your conclusion allows you to restate and tie together your main point, your arguments, or lines of analysis into one neat and tidy package. A good conclusion sticks to the major points made in your main paragraphs and leads to a logical outcome that the reader would expect. It should not, however, just be a restatement of your introduction. You've covered a lot of territory in your paper, so in the conclusion you want to remind your reader of your most compelling arguments and evidence.

The conclusion should also propel your readers into some further thoughts on your topic—leave 'em wanting more! The conclusion, however, isn't the place to start introducing new evidence, new material, or radically different ideas from what you've presented or to throw in some piece of fascinating information that you just discovered. It's the FINALE! The END!

OTHER PESKY PARTS: FOOTNOTES, ENDNOTES, AND LISTS OF SOURCES

Yes, we're back to these details. If your instructor really wants to put you through the paces of writing a research paper, he or she may insist on the inclusion of footnotes, either as citations for sources or as a way to add information or comments to enhance the text.

Footnotes

Use a footnote to cite a source. You may also use a footnote to include information that is not a major point of your argument but is something you'd like the reader to know. Footnotes may contain details that only the most avid reader will want to know.

If you need to use footnotes, you'll find that they are uniformly a pain in the neck, even if your word processing program allows you to enter them automatically. You need to get them on the same page as the text to which they relate; they must be numbered as superscripts consecutively throughout the document and be presented in the correct format.

Endnotes

Endnotes are easier to include in your paper than footnotes. Why? Because they can be tucked away at the end of a chapter or at the end of the paper itself. They are less convenient for your readers who'll have to do some page flipping around to read them, but from the writer's standpoint, they beat footnotes any day. They basically contain the same info as a footnote. They can be used for source citation or to include additional information for the interested reader. Although footnotes are usually single-spaced, endnotes are often double-spaced.

Lists of Sources

An important part of your research paper is the list of sources, proving you actually consulted something other than your buddies, blogs, and encyclopedias for your masterpiece. Depending on what your instructor requests and the style manual you're following, this list can vary slightly according to content.

Bibliography

The list of *all* sources that you consulted is technically a **bibliography.** You may or may not have cited every source in the text, but you still drew upon them to understand your topic. If your instructor requests an **annotated bibliography,** you need to write a summary sentence or two about each work and include that information with the citation.

Works Cited

If you're following the Modern Language Association style, you might be asked to include a list of "Works Cited." This list usually only reflects sources that you have actually cited in your text. You might have read *My Life as a Superhero* by Ace Biggerthanlife to get some background understanding for your paper on superheroes, but if you didn't quote, summarize, or paraphrase Ace or cite some material from his book, he's off your "Works Cited" list.

Reference List

Your instructor might also want your list of sources as a **reference list.** Ask him or her what sources should be cited here, as he or she might expect a full bibliography or only a Works Cited list.

USING YOUR AMMO TO PROVE YOUR POINT

By now, you've managed to put together some good thoughts in a coherent way. You next want to punch up your document with the research you've done to support your major points. Your paper needs to be more than one long list of quotations, other people's thoughts, or someone else's facts. If it's merely a string of quotations, summaries, or paraphrases that aren't unzipped into your own ideas, you'll flunk!

Getting back to our example about the Emperor penguins' relocation to Buenos Aires due to global warming, here's how to integrate information from an authority figure and several quotations to support a main paragraph idea.

The Emperor penguins' lives have improved in their new surroundings at the Buenos Aires zoo. Leading Emperor penguin researcher, Susan Bird, has found that the survival rates for newly hatched chicks has increased 10 percent, the average body weight of adult males and females has risen, and the penguins seem to enjoy their leisure time more (Bird 2007)[1]. Although some researchers say that the penguins are just growing fat and lazy at the zoo (Alcott 14; Cutter 27), none of them has presented conclusive evidence that the relocation has harmed the penguins in any way. Indeed, the penguins themselves only see positive benefits to their new situation: "Here at the zoo, we've got our own glacier floe and a spacious swimming area complete with climbing rocks," says Big Ernie, the troop's media relations expert. "In addition, we're fed three times a day and don't have to worry about an interrupted food supply. We've got all the fish we can eat! Another plus is that we can take tango lessons just in case they decide to use real penguins for a remake of the film Happy Feet.*" (Personal interview, January 6, 2007).*

For this species, the unexpected consequences of global warming continue to open new opportunities for them on the mainland. (Start of a new paragraph that continues to build the argument).

The paragraph topic sentence is supported by a summary of evidence from a well-known scholar, opposing views are acknowledged, and a direct interview with an official spokes-penguin is used to cement your assertion that the penguins' lives have improved. A supporting quotation for your point is integrated

---

[1] Dr. Susan Bird is the leading authority on Emperor penguins. She spent twenty-five years on the ice floes of the Antarctica studying all facets of their existence before following the penguins to Buenos Aires when they finally decided to relocate. Her book, *What I Don't Know About Emperor Penguins Isn't Worth Knowing,* is the seminal work on this species.

into the paragraph. The footnote gives the reader additional information about the world authority on this species. All sources are appropriately acknowledged by in-text citations, which will be detailed in the bibliography or Works Cited page. The transition words "although" and "indeed" carry the reader through the text.

Remember: Your job is to give an explanation of the idea you are presenting, back it up with evidence (quotations, statistics, and so on), and make some comment on what the evidence means or why it is of value. It's your job to interpret your evidence and show its relevance to the point you're making.

REVISING YOUR FIRST DRAFT

Okay, it may not be great, but it's down on paper! Even the best writers don't get it just right on the first draft. That's why it's called a draft. It's your first stab at pulling your research together and making your argument and analysis.

Now it's time for the editing and revising of your work. Your main goal in revising your first draft is to make sure that your main idea is well stated and supported with sufficient evidence and that your argument or analysis hangs together and flows well. Ideas and structure are your focus. At this point, pay attention to grammatical and spelling errors, but don't obsess about them. Correct them as you see them, but leave the fine detail work for the final proofreading stage. Don't sweat the small stuff now; sweat the big stuff.

Print out your draft so that you can read it as a whole, without the temptation to try to make changes or corrections as you go along. Mark up your draft with your thoughts and then make changes. Reorganize where you need to reorganize; pump up your supporting arguments or evidence where they are weak.

Here are some questions to ask yourself as you read your first draft:

- Is my introduction an attention-grabber that states my thesis completely?

- In the body of my paper, does each paragraph have one main idea that I develop and support sufficiently with evidence from my research?

- Have I linked the paragraphs logically, and do they each relate directly to my thesis?

ZIP TIPS

Hardly anyone writes a paper that's perfect in every way on the first try. Put aside your masterpiece for a day or two before your head explodes and then tackle revisions.

- Have I made my argument or analysis in a logical fashion? Can someone else clearly follow my line of thinking?

- Have I taken the assignment and audience into account with my writing style and tone?

- Based on the material I've presented, does my conclusion make sense?

- How can I make this draft better? Better organization of material? Deletion of some material? More evidence? Better use of evidence?

UNZIPPING RIGHT ALONG

- Review and analyze your research. By reading through it again, you'll continue to pull out major points, fill in your outline, and stimulate your creative juices for the writing process.

ZIP TIPS

Ask someone else to read your first draft and give you some feedback. It might make sense to you, but here's a real test to see if it's clear to your audience.

- Focus on pulling your ideas and research together into a coherent and logical paper where each paragraph supports your analysis or argument.

- Be sure that your writing is crisp and clear and that the words you choose convey what you really mean.

- If you're stuck and can't get the words out, give yourself a break and just stop. A few minutes of mindless television, a walk, or an instant message to a friend won't totally grind the process to a halt.

HIDDEN SNAGS

- Patting yourself on the back for finishing your paper, even though it reads like someone took a machete to it! You forgot the first go-round isn't necessarily the last. Reread and revise!

- Lapsing into slang or using e-mail shortcuts instead of standard English. Save your smiley faces for your friends!

- Failing to stick to the point of your research paper, which is to analyze or argue a point and not just to summarize what you've researched and read and tack on an introduction and conclusion.

- Assuming that your audience is a bunch of dolts who need to have every word and idea explained to them in excruciating detail. It clogs up your writing and the brains of your readers with unnecessary information and also insults them.

MORE TO UNZIP

It takes a lot of work, especially organization, to reach the point where you're ready to start to write your paper. As you review your materials and pull your paper together, you'll be able to see how your evidence fits together best to state your case and where your thinking is fuzzy. This is the time to get the big stuff right. You'll attend to the finer details in the next round of refinement.

You may choose to try to zip through the entire first draft in one sitting, just to empty your head onto paper, and then go back and fill in the blanks. Or you may prefer to tackle your paper one piece at a time. It's up to you how you proceed. Just leave yourself enough time to get a second opinion, put aside the draft for a while to clear your mind, and revise the paper with attention to your style, tone, audience, and the main point you want to make. You're almost done!

HOOK ME UP TO MORE RESOURCES

- **http://writing-program.uchicago.edu/resources/collegewriting,** has excellent information about the overall writing process.

- **http://owl.english.purdue.edu** offers great advice about the writing process, parts of the research paper, and links to more resources on every topic discussed in this chapter.

CHAPTER 7

Citing Sources:
It's a Big Deal

JUST LIKE OTHER inventors, writers want credit for their work, and they don't want you to claim it as yours when it isn't. Plagiarism, or stealing someone else's work, is a big deal. Plagiarism can get you suspended or kicked out of school or college, or worse. Knowing how and when to cite sources appropriately will help you sidestep this potential snag in your academic career.

This chapter reveals:

- Ethics Involved in Research

- Ways to Sort Out Right from Wrong

- The Downside of Not Doing Your Own Work

WHAT'S THE BIG DEAL WITH PLAGIARISM?

Think about the famous name clothing and handbag designers whose very expensive products are reproduced cheaply as "knock offs" and passed off as originals for a fraction of the cost. This activity infringes on their design ideas and trademarks and costs them millions of dollars. It's also against the law.

Plagiarism is similar, only it refers to the theft of ideas and words or products of the mind. Plagiarism is taking, using, or presenting others' works and ideas as your own without appropriate acknowledgement of the source of the information. If you plagiarize, you may also violate copyright laws that exist to protect all kinds of intellectual property ranging from books and music to photographs and videos.

Plagiarism is a big deal to your instructors because it is involves academic dishonesty, as well as theft of intellectual property. From the academic standpoint, it's a form of cheating because you're basically not doing your own work. Think about it this way: Would you want to work hard on a paper, original idea, or experiment and then have someone else take the credit for it? Of course not.

DO THE RIGHT THING

A lot of grief can be avoided by following some simple rules of thumb. Here are the types of materials that always need to be acknowledged:

- Someone else's ideas, opinions, or theory

ZIP TIPS

Make sure you read a copy of your school's policy on plagiarism and follow its guidelines when writing your papers. Your instructor may also include a statement about plagiarism in the course outline or syllabus.

- Facts and statistics that are not considered to be common knowledge

- An author's interpretations of facts

- An author's argument or line of thinking

- Actual quotations, written or spoken (such as from an interview)

- Unique or distinctive phrases

- A summary or paraphrase of someone else's words or ideas

- Graphics such as diagrams, illustrations, charts, pictures, and other visual materials

- Audios, videos, or other electronic material that you didn't produce

Fair Use and Copyrighted Material

Many works are protected by copyrights that give individuals the exclusive right to distribute and reproduce their material. There are laws about what can be legitimately borrowed or used from such works without getting prior written consent from the author. In the United States, there is a concept called "fair use" in copyright law that lists purposes for which reproduction of a copyrighted work might be considered "fair." For academic purposes, using a short quotation with appropriate citation for teaching, scholarship, and research purposes is generally considered to be "fair use."

Read a publisher's statement about fair use and copyright permission carefully. It only takes a letter to the copyright owner to ask for permission to use copyrighted material, but this may also take time that you don't have. Unless you're publishing your research paper, you probably won't need written permission, but if there's any doubt, ask your instructor.

Yikes! Is anything out there that can be used freely and not be considered to be plagiarism? Will my term paper be one gigantic citation?

Common Knowledge

Yes, there are some facts that can be used without acknowledgement. Common knowledge is a fact that can be documented in several

ZIP TIPS

Ideas, quotes, graphics, visuals, and other materials from the World Wide Web follow the same rules of plagiarism as printed material.

reference sources and is generally known by many people. For example, "President Bill Clinton was the 42nd president of the United States," "The earth's circumference is approximately 25,000 miles," and "Leonardo DaVinci painted the Mona Lisa" are facts that are commonly known and can be documented in several reference sources.

A fact as specific as "Thirty-five percent of all superheroes quit their jobs by the time they are 40" would not be considered common knowledge, would appear to be based on a special study, and would have to be documented.

Public Domain

Some documents have never been copyrighted or their copyright has expired. They are considered to be in the public domain, that is, accessible to the public. United States government publications are examples of documents that are considered to be in the public domain (unless they are classified documents) and can be used freely without fear of infringing on a copyright. Of course, even when documents are in the public domain, you will still have to cite these sources correctly.

Stuff Right Out of Your Head

Anything that is your original idea and that you personally produce, such as artwork, photographs, a CD-ROM, a movie, a report based on your original laboratory experiments or fieldwork, and your own observations, thoughts, and ideas about a topic are yours.

WHY CITE?

A citation is the information that shows the origin of material from an external source, whether it's a quotation, someone else's idea, your paraphrase, and so on.

- Correct citations are good defenses against plagiarism because you are both giving credit where credit is due and giving the reader specific information about the original source of the material.

- Citations also let your instructor and others know that you've done your homework by digging into appropriate sources. They offer external authoritative support and evidence for your arguments or findings.

ZIP TIPS

It's hard to believe that you could plagiarize yourself, but if you submitted the same research paper to two different classes, you've basically self-plagiarized.

- Citations also allow anyone who is interested to follow-up on those sources you've cited, in case they're interested in learning more about the topic that you've sweated over in your paper.

HOW TO CITE RIGHT

There are several common ways to document sources: **direct quotations, in-text parenthetical citations, footnotes** and **endnotes,** and the **bibliography.** Yes, it would be great to cite your sources only in your bibliography, but then your reader has no way of associating the source to a specific passage in your paper. In addition, the bibliography does not contain information about the specific pages where you got the information.

Direct Quotations

This is easy. Simply put quotations around the *exact* words you are incorporating into your paper. Remember to use ellipses if you

ZIP TIPS

You need to put appropriate citations within the text of your paper AND show the complete source in your bibliography.

leave out information or square brackets if you add a word to clarify something. Don't, however, add anything to the quote that would change the quotation's meaning.

In-Text Parenthetical Citation (also called Author-Date Citation)

This is an easy way to refer to your source within the text of your paper. Depending on how you state the information, this type of citation usually requires only the author's last name, the date of publication, and the page or pages from which you took the material.

Of course, each style manual has a preferred way to format the citation, and there are many variations on the theme, so you need to consult the style sheet handed out by your instructor or the style manual designated for use.

The Modern Language Association (MLA) requires the author's name and the page number; if there is more than one text per author in the bibliography (MLA calls this Works Cited), you also include the title of the work.

> *In his book, The Lives of Superheroes, Ace Biggerthanlife suggests that superheroes lead difficult lives and are subject to burnout just like the rest of us (79).*

> *One superhero sums it up: "Life as a superhero isn't easy." (Biggerthanlife 79).*

If there were more than one source for Biggerthanlife, you would include the name of the text also (e.g., Biggerthanlife, The Lives of Superheroes, 79) to identify the book from which the material originates.

In MLA style, if you're referring to the entire text rather than to a specific passage, just include the author's name in the sentence rather than using a parenthetical citation.

> *Ace Biggerthanlife examines the pros and cons of being a superhero.*

The Chicago Manual of Style would cite that same material as follows:

> *According to Ace Biggerthanlife, superheroes lead difficult lives and are subject to burnout just like the rest of us (2007, 79).*

> *One superhero sums it up: "Life as a superhero isn't easy." (Biggerthanlife 2007, 79)*

The American Psychological Association offers this format:

> *According to Ace Biggerthanlife (2007), superheroes lead difficult lives and are subject to burnout just like the rest of us (p. 79).*

> *One superhero sums it up: "Life as a superhero isn't easy." (Biggerthanlife, 2007, p. 79).*

Footnotes and Endnotes

These can also be used as source citations, but they are placed outside the text of the document. Footnotes are located at the bottom of the page with a superscript, and endnotes are located at the end of the paper, usually designated with a number. *The Chicago Manual of Style* gives you the alternative of citing works in the text as just shown or of citing them using a footnote or an endnote.

In the text, you would add a superscript number at the end of the passage:

> *According to Ace Biggerthanlife, superheroes lead difficult lives and are subject to burnout just like the rest of us[1].*

To use a footnote for citation purposes, you would place your footnote at the bottom of the same page where the text or idea is cited. Your footnote would include the number, author's first and last name, title, (place of publication: publisher, date), and page number. Footnotes are consecutively numbered.

> [1]Ace Biggerthanlife, *The Lives of Superheroes*. (New York: Outofsight Books, 2007), 79.

If you were using endnotes at the end of the paper, they would include the same information and formatting as the footnote and be consecutively numbered 1, 2, 3, and so on. Endnote numbers do not appear as superscripts.

Bibliography (also called References or Works Cited)

When there is a citation in a text, you must include the complete information about that source in the bibliography at the end of your paper. Otherwise, readers will not be able to relate the citation to a particular source. Makes sense, right?

The MLA bibliographic reference for our superhero book would read:

> Biggerthanlife, Ace. <u>The Lives of Superheroes</u>. New York: OutofSight Books, 2007.

PLAGIARISM OR NOT?

Here are some examples from our fictional book, *The Lives of Superheroes*, to help you sort out whether or not something is plagiarism.

Original Quote:

> *In his famous work,* The Lives of Superheroes, *Ace Bigger-thanlife said, "Life as a superhero isn't easy. People have expectations, and it is the responsibility of superheroes to live up to those expectations. Superheroes accept their re-sponsibilities gladly, but sometimes wish they could have a day off just like everyone else. When the demands get to be too much, sometimes they just give up. In the business, this phenomenon is called superhero burn-out." (79)*

Plagiarized Quote:

> *In his book,* The Lives of Superheroes, *Ace Biggerthanlife says that "Life as a superhero isn't easy." People have ex-*

> *pectations, and it is the responsibility of superheroes to live up to those expectations. Superheroes accept their responsibilities gladly, but sometimes wish they could have a day off just like everyone else. When the demands get to be too much, sometimes they just give up. In the business, this phenomenon is called superhero burn-out. (79)*

Why? Even though page number 79 is cited (and presumably the book's information is cited in the bibliography), you only put quotations around the first part of the quotation and then copied the next lines word for word without acknowledging the source. Quotation marks need to go around the entire quote.

Plagiarized Text:

> *As anyone can imagine, life as a superhero isn't easy. Superheroes bear a lot of responsibility trying to meet everyone's expectations, which they are happy to do. They too occasionally need a break from their responsibilities. Otherwise, they can suffer from superhero burn-out.*

Why? For several reasons. First, you still copied a line directly from the text, "Life as a superhero isn't easy" without putting it in quotation marks. Even though you paraphrased the rest of the text adequately, you also failed to put quotation marks around "superhero burn-out," which could be considered to be a distinctive or unique phrase. It came directly from the book and mind of Ace Biggerthanlife, so it should be set off in quotes. There is also no citation to show where the text came from or to relate it to a source in the bibliography.

THE DOWNSIDE OF NOT DOING YOUR OWN WORK

Most high schools, colleges, and universities have academic codes of conduct that spell out how students should behave at school and in the classroom. Plagiarism is usually a prominent part of those codes of conducts with the consequences clearly spelled out. It's right up there with drug abuse, drinking on campus, unruly behavior, and other forms of bad behavior that can get you kicked out of class or off the campus. Saying "I didn't know" doesn't hold much water when your instructor has given you a written guide, including punishments, about plagiarism.

Penalties for plagiarism in academic settings can include:

- A failing grade in the class

- Requirement to re-take a class

ZIP TIPS

When in doubt, include a citation or check with your instructor. Better to be safe than sorry! One more citation isn't going to hurt, but an accusation of plagiarism will.

- Academic probation

- Expulsion from school

Bottom line: It's better and safer to know the rules about plagiarism and to avoid it by acknowledging and documenting sources properly.

UNZIPPING RIGHT ALONG

- When in doubt, it's better to cite a source and/or check with your instructor. Librarians can be helpful on this issue also.

- Follow your instructor's directions about the preferred style for citations.

- When taking notes, check them against the original text to be sure you've copied a quotation accurately and that you haven't just changed a word or two if you're summarizing or paraphrasing.

- Keep multiple drafts of your paper in case other students who might be less honest are tempted to lift your work and present it as their own (yes, it happens).

HIDDEN SNAGS

- Letting another student persuade you that it's okay for him or her to use a paper you've already written or that it's okay for you to use another student's work or to buy a paper from an online paper mill. It's still plagiarism!

- Thinking that you can sidestep citations by listing all your sources in the bibliography. They need to be in the text with the passage you quote, paraphrase, or summarize.

- Pasting passages from Web pages directly into the working draft of your paper opens up the door to confusion. You'll forget where you got the info or not remember if it was your idea or someone else's. It could cause a big headache later on.

HOOK ME UP TO MORE RESOURCES

- For more about the issue of copyright and fair use, see **http://www.copyright.gov/fls/fl102.html.**

- If you need to obtain permission to use copyrighted material, Springfield Township High School's Online Research Guide offers a good example of a letter request at **http://www.sdst.org/rguide.**

- Bedford St. Martin's *Online!* at **http://www.bedfordst martins.com/online/citex.html** is an excellent resource for Internet source citation drawing on the guides listed here, as well as other style manuals.

- *Publication Manual of the American Psychological Association,* 5th ed. Washington, D.C.: American Psychological Association, 2001.

- *The Chicago Manual of Style: The Essential Guide for Writers, Editors, and Publishers,* 15th ed. Chicago, IL: University of Chicago Press, 2003.

- *MLA Style Manual and Guide to Scholarly Publishing,* 2nd ed. Edited by Joseph Gibaldi. New York: Modern Language Association of America, 1998.

MORE TO UNZIP

Writing a research paper is serious stuff. You need to be sure that what's yours is yours and what's someone else's has been acknowledged appropriately. You can inadvertently get yourself in a heap of trouble by not understanding the concept of plagiarism or by deciding that the rules don't apply to you just because you're in high school or college. Don't kid yourself! Instructors and educational institutions take plagiarism very seriously, because ideas and words are what they produce. Plagiarism not only steals a product, it tramples on a time-honored code of conduct and behavior in academic institutions. It's best to avoid even the suspicion of plagiarism. You can do that by understanding what it is, taking careful notes, and using citations to document your sources.

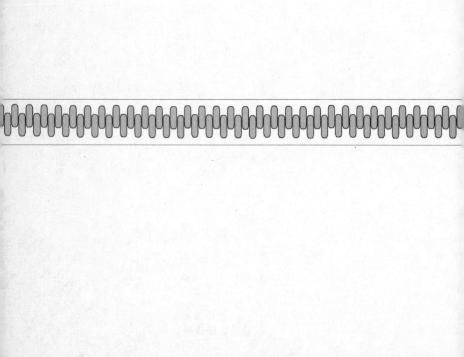

CHAPTER 8

Ah—Totally Unzipped

AH! THE FINAL draft at last! Your unzipped mind has nearly completed its process of creating the perfect research paper. Now, it's time to zip it up with some double and triple checks to make sure everything hangs together, is spelled correctly, and bears a strong resemblance to standard English.

Would you want to read a ten-page paper in which SpongeBob is spelled wrong a hundred times? Of course not, and neither does your instructor. You'll also want to be sure that your final paper does not look like your printer chewed it up and spit it out in one final act of vengeance. Looks count!

This chapter reveals:

- The Path to Presentation Perfection

- Common Goofs in Grammar, Spelling, Punctuation, and Word Usage

- Techniques for Avoiding and Coping with Catastrophes

IT'S FINISHED: THE FINAL FORMAT

Your final version should be a masterpiece of presentation laid out in the time-honored order of front matter, body, and end matter.

Front Matter

You'll need to introduce your paper with some materials before the body of the paper called front matter. Depending on its length and complexity, the front matter may include, in this order:

- Title page

- Table of contents

- Foreword (an introduction usually written by an expert, not you)

- Preface (where you acknowledge those who have helped you)

- Abstract

Note that it's unlikely that you'll need either a foreword or preface for a high school or undergraduate research paper.

Title Page

Your title page should include the following information at a minimum:

- Title of the paper

- Your name

- Date

- Your instructor's name and the class for which the paper was written

Table of Contents

The table of contents reflects the major sections of your paper and should follow directly from your outline.

Foreword

If you need one, find an expert on your paper's topic, and ask him or her to make a statement that your paper is the next best thing to sliced bread.

Preface

Here's your chance at an Oscar acceptance speech in writing. Thank everyone who has contributed in some significant way to your masterpiece. Be sure to spell their names correctly.

Abstract

Again, this may not be necessary, but your instructor may ask you to include one. The abstract should be several sentences that summarize your research paper. Whoever reads it should be able to grasp what your paper is about without having to read the whole thing.

Body of the Paper

Well, this is basically the research paper itself with well-written paragraphs and numbered pages.

End Matter

End matter zips up your paper with the bibliography or Works Cited pages, any additional material that might not fit within the text itself, such as a chart, a graph, or a glossary of terms with which the reader may be unfamiliar. End matter that follows the bibliography often goes in lettered appendices.

LOOKS AND NEATNESS COUNT

After you've worked this hard, you don't want to turn in a paper that looks like something the dog just dragged in from the garbage can. On the other hand, a great-looking presentation can't make up for the fact that you didn't follow the assignment or do the required research. So do your work *and* turn in a neat, clean, and well-proofed paper that follows your instructor's directions for presentation.

Some good rules of thumb for presentation are:

- Neatly type and print out your paper on clean, good quality, white 8 ½" × 11" paper

- Set margins of 1 inch on all sides. Do not justify the right margin.

- Put a header with your name and the page number on each page of the body of the paper.

- Double or single space the body depending on the format instructions you've been given. Long quotations are usually single-spaced and indented.

- Use an easily readable font, such as 11- or 12-point Times New Roman or Arial.

- Start your bibliography (references or Works Cited) on a separate page. Appendices begin on separate pages also.

- Follow the appropriate style manual for the format of quotations, footnotes, endnotes, and reference material, as well as for abbreviations, capitalization, and use of numbers.

- Depending on your instructor's preferences, staple or clip the paper or insert it into a simple folder (with a label showing at least your name and title page).

ZIP TIPS

Be sure that the page numbers on your table of contents match the page numbers of your paper, especially if you've made changes and printed it out several times.

WATCH THAT GRAMMAR, SPELLING, AND WORD CHOICE!

There may be occasions when proper grammar, spelling, and appropriate use of words don't particularly matter. This isn't one of them. Instructors don't want to read sentences with mismatched nouns and verbs, incorrectly used words, improper spelling, and so on. These errors really detract from your content. Your instructor might even take off points for these items, so clean up your paper.

Write It Right

Here are some basic points of grammar to remember:

- Subjects and verbs need to agree.

    Single Noun, Single Verb: The student is sitting down.

    Plural Noun, Plural Verb: The students are sitting down.

- Pronouns and nouns need to be in sync. Singular pronouns are used to refer to singular nouns; plural pronouns refer to plural nouns.

    Out-of-sync: If a student buys a book at the bookstore, they receive a discount.

    In-sync: If a student buys a book at the bookstore, he or she receives a discount.

    If students buy books at the book store, they receive a discount.

    Remember words such as *anyone, anything, each,*

everyone, nothing, whoever, nobody, and *none* are singular and require single verbs.

- Verb tenses should be consistent.

    Inconsistent: She went to the store and then returns home. (This mixes the past tense with the present tense.)

    Consistent: She went to the store and then returned home.

- Complete sentences have a subject and a verb; otherwise, they are a fragment.

- The internal sentence structure of words, phrases, or clauses needs to be parallel.

    Non-parallel: Bill found that he could not juggle his work schedule, attending school, and playing sports.

    Parallel: Bill found that he could not juggle his work schedule, school, and sports.

    Non-parallel: Beth told her mother that she was going to school and playing tennis later.

    Parallel: Beth told her mother *that* she was going to school and *that* she was playing tennis later.

- Use correct word placement to ensure clarity. There's a big difference between "The instructor tripped on the student and fell" and "The instructor tripped and fell on the student."

Spell It Rite—Uh, Right

Misspelled words can make even the most interesting research paper maddening to read. They make your paper look sloppy. They can change the meaning of a sentence, because a misspelled word is often a misused word.

If you are not a good speller, have someone who is a good speller read and correct your spelling. Of course, you can use your word processor to do an initial run-through, but if you can't spell you still won't know whether or not the word is spelled correctly for its context. Even if you can spell, word processors only correct misspelled words. If you meant to say, "I heard something of interest" and you spelled it "I herd something of interest," the spell checker won't pick up the error because "herd" is spelled correctly.

Even if you're an excellent speller, double-check your work as typos do creep in. Sometimes, words just look funny although you've used them a hundred times. When in doubt, look up the word and its proper meaning and use in the dictionary.

Use Those Words Correctly

Improper word use also drives instructors nuts. There are zillions of words that are often confused or misused. Here are ten that you don't want to trip over.

1. *All together* and *altogether.*
   All together means that everybody or everything is in a group: *The students gathered all together in the library to begin their research. Altogether* means

completely or on the whole: *Six o'clock in the morning is altogether too early to leave for school.*

2. *Among* and *between.*
   Use *among* when you are discussing three or more people, places, or things. Use *between* when there are only two people, places, or things involved.

3. *Compose* and *comprise.*
   The parts *compose* the whole, and the whole *comprises* the parts. *Compose* means to create or put together: *Four men and eight women compose* (or make up) *the jury. Comprise* means to contain, consist of, or to include all: *The book comprises eight chapters.* If you can change *comprises* to *consists of,* then you are using it correctly.

4. *Here* and *hear.*
   Here is an adverb indicating place. *Hear* is a verb that means to discern sound or listen.

5. *It's* and *its.*
   The first is a contraction of it is; the second is a possessive pronoun showing ownership. *It's a big deal to get an "A" in Professor Excellent's course. The school notes its policy on plagiarism on its Web site.*

6. *Principal* and *principle.*
   The *principal* is the big cheese at your high school,

the head, the chief, or an investment. A *principle* is
a law, rule, or doctrine: *It's not the money; it's the
principle of the thing!*

7. *Sit* and *set.*
   People *sit.* Things *set* or are *set. Jack sits on the floor
   when he watches television. Jack set the magazine
   on the table.*

8. *Than* and *then.*
   Than is used to make comparisons: *She is older than
   her brother. Then* means at that time or in the case
   of: *She couldn't wait until then. If she wanted to go
   out, then she'd have to do the dishes.*

9. *There, their,* and *they're.*
   There is an adverb showing location; *their* is a
   possessive pronoun showing ownership; and *they're*
   is a contraction of *they are. They're waiting for their
   friends to arrive at the gate over there.*

10. *Wear* and *where.*
    Wear means to have on clothes or to diminish
    through use: *He wears up-to-date fashions. The gold
    leaf is wearing away. Where* denotes place: *The
    cafeteria is where we eat lunch.*

YES, COMMAS ARE A BIG DEAL

Instructors also admire and expect the appropriate use of
punctuation throughout your research paper. If you've forgotten
basic punctuation skills, here's a short primer:

- A period signals the end of a complete thought.

- A semi-colon links two related sentences.

- A colon introduces a list of items.

- Quotation marks appear at the beginning and end of quotations.

- An apostrophe shows possession or indicates a contraction.

Commas are tricky and have been the source of much debate, because at times they are overused and seem to appear everywhere.

- Commas separate dependent clauses from independent clauses in sentences: *When Beth finished studying, she decided to walk the dog.*

- Commas separate items in lists; traditional use dictates that a comma appears before the connecting word in the list: *Ben used green, red, blue, and purple index cards for his notes.*

FINAL, FINAL REVISION

Take one more look at your research paper to check for consistency of thought and flow. Does everything make sense? Are there any awkward sentences that could be restructured to read more smoothly? Is each paragraph linked to the one immediately before and after with a good transition sentence? Is the topic of each paragraph clear? Is there enough evidence to "hold up" your assertion in each paragraph and the overall point you're making in the paper? Are the style and tone appropriate for your audience, and are they consistent throughout the paper? Make any final tune-ups and then send it on to the proofreaders: yourself and someone who really likes you and is literate.

PROOF AND PROOF AGAIN

Set your final version aside for a while before you proof it for the first time. Once you're ready, look for errors of grammar, spelling, and word use as well as for typos. Also watch out for formatting errors, missing letters, pages where words have been cut off or where sentences don't flow to the next page, spacing, and so on. Be sure to proofread your bibliography or Works Cited page, endnotes, footnotes, captions, and graphic material. When you proofread, forget about the content of the paper, and focus on the details.

Proofreading your paper once won't be enough. You'll catch new errors each time you go through it. Try to review it at least three times, and get at least one outside reader to go over it. Make the necessary corrections each time, and print out a new copy of your paper each time that you review it.

WHEN DISASTER STRIKES

We've all had that sinking feeling in the pit of our stomachs that "Uh oh, maybe I hit Delete instead of Save," only to find out that yes, the final version of the document has been swallowed up by the computer gods for good. Even though everyone tells you nothing is ever deleted from your hard drive, it doesn't matter when it is 4 a.m., your tech-geek roommate isn't around, and your paper is due at 8 a.m.

Of course, you also neglected to follow the first cardinal rule of writing: Always back up your document! Always print out a copy of your paper at various stages, because you never know when your computer is going to turn on you and decide not to surrender your latest version.

But what do you do now? If you have good notes and a decent draft of the almost-completed final version, get to work. You'll have a good shot at getting close to the final version—if you don't fall asleep first.

ZIP TIPS

Recruit another pair of eyeballs to help proof your paper. Someone who hasn't spent 12 hours finalizing a paper can see errors that you'll overlook because you're in a daze.

If you have to throw yourself on the mercy of your instructor, bring proof that you've been working diligently—notes, a draft bibliography, and the less-than-perfect version of the paper. You might be able to buy yourself an extra day or two, especially if you've been a reliable student up to this point. Instructors have heard it all and have a fine ear for the truth versus a whopper of a lie.

Don't throw in the towel and buy a paper online.

UNZIPPING RIGHT ALONG

- Edit and proofread your paper more than once to be sure it flows logically, has smooth transitions, and is as error-free as you can make it. Take as much care proofreading the paper's front and end matter as the body of the paper.

- Consult the dictionary, thesaurus, grammar books, and style manuals to be sure your paper sounds and looks good.

- Make a backup copy of each version of your research paper. Print out each version just in case your computer decides to send your paper into a black hole.

HIDDEN SNAGS

- Printing out and handing in the wrong version of your document. Make sure that the final version is indeed the final version!

- Relying only on the word processing spelling and grammar checker to proof your document. The word processor can tell you whether or not a word is spelled incorrectly, but it can't discern whether or not a word is used correctly.

- Waiting until the last minute to finish your paper and realizing that you're three pages short of—or five pages over—the limit. You won't have time to make adjustments.

- Using a large font to meet the required page length. Instructors are on to that one.

- Forgetting to include your name on the title page of the paper or on the body of the paper. Your instructor may be able to guess who wrote it, but don't count on it.

HOOK ME UP TO MORE RESOURCES

- For help with the basics of grammar and style, check out the time-honored classic, *The Elements of Style* by William Strunk, Jr. and E.B. White. 4th ed. Boston: Allyn and Bacon, 2000.

- If you really need to beef up your punctuation skills, check out *Better Punctuation in 30 Minutes a Day,* by Ceil Cleveland. Franklin Lakes, NJ: The Career Press, 2002.

- **http://www.merriam-webster.com** is where you can look up words in both the dictionary and the thesaurus.

- **http://www.owl.english.purdue.edu/handouts/grammar** has rules of grammar, punctuation, and spelling plus exercises.

- **http://homepage.smc.edu/reading_lab/words_commonly_ confused.htm** has a list of words that are easily confused and exercises to test your knowledge about their meaning and use.

MORE TO UNZIP

Getting your research masterpiece into its final form requires concentrated effort and attention to detail. It's the little things that can kill you, such as inadvertently replacing every reference to "Freud" with "Fred" and not catching the error. Your instructor will not be amused (well, he or she actually will be, but the oversight may cost you more than embarrassment).

While looks aren't everything, your thoughts do deserve a nice setting, so pay attention to the basics of presentation. Turn in a neatly organized, well-proofed paper. Your instructor will be able to concentrate on your ideas, argument, or analysis without the distraction of trying to read through the coffee stains on each page. Your paper will look as brilliant as it truly is, you'll wow and zow your instructor, you'll get an "A," and life will once again be good because you've mastered the art of the research paper.

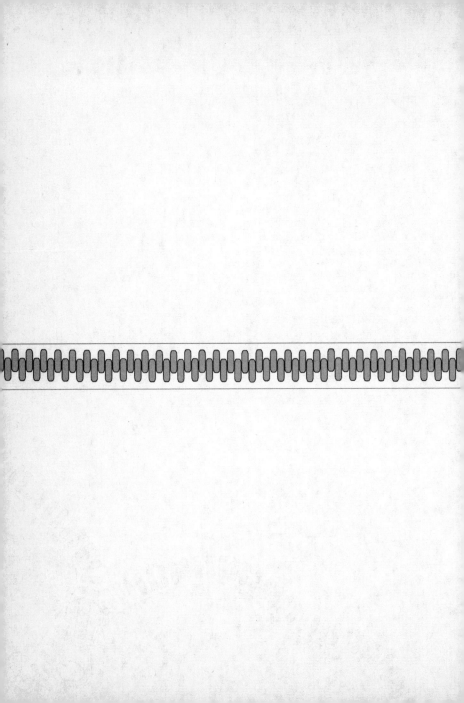

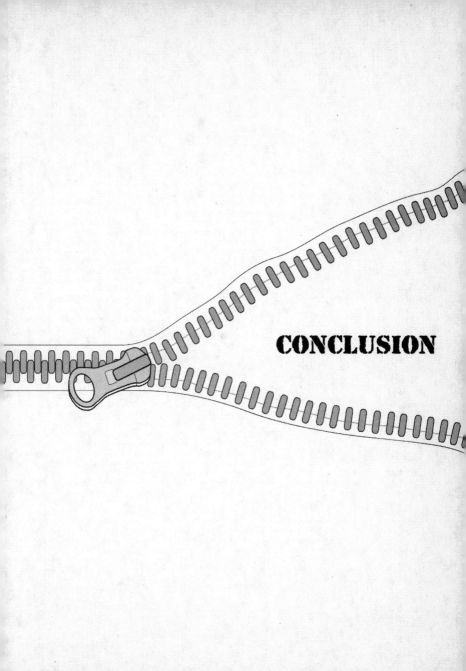

CONCLUSION

WHEW! YOU MADE it through reading about the process of writing a research paper, and you've lived to tell the tale. Give yourself a pat on the back and zip out to do something fun. When you come back, you'll still have that research paper to write, but now you have a good understanding of what is involved and how to succeed.

This book and the resources cited are all here to back you up as you twirl potential topics around in your head, tailor that topic to the specifications of the assignment, and take the plunge into the library to start your research. Unzip your mind, leave yourself open to the adventure, and give yourself enough time to do the assignment. If you get hung up, get help whenever you need it and from whatever sources are available to inspire you and to get unstuck—online assistance, your instructor or teaching assistant, a writing tutor, or this book.

Remember knowing how to make an argument or tackle a research question, how to research and organize information, and how to present it in a clear and coherent way are all skills that will serve you well in the future. And, the more papers you write, the better you'll get at writing them.

Now, consider yourself unzipped with the power to tackle that research paper, avoid the hidden snags, and unzip right along from the start to the finish. Go for it!